Tales from the Tinny

Tales from the Tinny

Get a Mullet Up Ya!

Rob Smith

ABC
Books

The ABC 'Wave' device is a trademark of the Australian Broadcasting Corporation and is used under licence by HarperCollins*Publishers* Australia.

First published in Australia in 2012
by HarperCollins*Publishers* Australia Pty Limited
ABN 36 009 913 517
harpercollins.com.au

HarperCollins*Publishers*
Level 13, 201 Elizabeth Street, Sydney NSW 2000, Australia
31 View Road, Glenfield, Auckland 0627, New Zealand
A 53, Sector 57, Noida, UP, India
77–85 Fulham Palace Road, London W6 8JB, United Kingdom
2 Bloor Street East, 20th floor, Toronto, Ontario M4W 1A8, Canada
10 East 53rd Street, New York NY 10022, USA

National Library of Australia Cataloguing-in-Publication entry:

Smith, Robert A. (Robert Allan)
Tales from the tinny : get a mullet up ya! / Robert Smith.
978 0 7333 3040 7 (pbk.)
978 0 7304 9834 6 (ebook)
Fishing – Northern Territory – Anecdotes.
Boats and boating – Northern Territory – Anecdotes.
Northern Territory – Social life and customs – Anecdotes.
Australian Broadcasting Corporation.
799.1099429

Cover design by raftcommunications.com.au
Cover image courtesy of the author
Typeset in Minion Pro by Kirby Jones

This book is dedicated to the valiant and noble fisher folk of the Top End.

Erudite and forthright, innovative and contemplative, great thinkers and great drinkers, we in the Tinny salute you fishos – we salute you one and all.

Contents

Manifesto

G'DAY, MY NAME is Robert Smith. Every Saturday morning from five, my crusty cohort Timothy Moore and I launch ABC Local Radio's *Tales from The Tinny* onto the Territory airwaves and the world wide web with a resounding splash. Tim and I stand tall and proud on the foredeck, casting about willy-nilly with rod in hand but not much in mind, while producer Mario (MC Fadge) Faggion mans bilge and tiller and miraculously keeps the whole thing afloat and somewhat on course.

Tim and I like to think of ourselves as observers and commentators on the myriad magnificent complexities of the human condition, viewed through the prism of a 'fisho's eye lens'. We provide pause for thought on matters profound and perplexing, puerile and politically improper. We see ourselves as humble facilitators of fishy discussion and conduits for the dissemination of angling insights.

There are others who regard us as nothing more than a couple of obnoxious boofheads with access to an electronic soapbox from which to launch a weekly spray of angling-based inanity – the truth of the matter probably lies somewhere in between.

While The Tinny maintains a central, fishy focus, we regularly range widely and tangentially into the realms of the irrelevant, the unrelated and the utterly ridiculous – thereby emulating the conversational flow aboard the beat-up, bait-encrusted, aluminium dinghies from which the show takes its name.

So when Tim and I are asked the standard conversational ice-breaker, 'What's your show about?', any explanation that would accurately encapsulate The Tinny would also grossly exceed the accepted standard duration for polite BBQ banter. We therefore generally settle on the broadly accurate, but suitably vague, '*Tales from The Tinny* is a show about fishing … sort of.'

In much the same way, if you consulted a dictionary for a concise description of fishing, you might find something along the lines of 'the activity of catching fish – either as food or for sport'.

Here too, the facts of the matter have been grossly oversimplified, for fishing is *so much more* than such a dry, condensed definition. Fishing is hopes and dreams, the inner journey and the seeking of enlightenment. It's about seeing fantastic country you'd never clap eyes on if you didn't have a rod in your hand. It's about spending long, contemplative hours on the water with a few mates and using that time to comprehensively thrash out the vexing, visceral issues of life itself – politics, theology, philosophy … and the bonkability rating of various tennis players and pop stars. It's about speaking outrageous rivers of rubbish and acting the grade-A galah. It's about the absolute disregard for socially acceptable levels of profanity and personal hygiene. It's about camaraderie, courage, cunning – and cold beer. Then, occasionally – more occasionally for some than others – it's even about catching fish!

Now, the catching of fish – though the stated aim of the exercise – is, of course, a purely serendipitous bonus. If it was the sole objective of proceedings, a cost–benefit analysis would quickly and clearly show the price per kilo of fish fillets to be so prohibitive that you would immediately liquidate all angling assets in a fire sale of financial harm minimisation.

On those heady occasions when we do actually bag a feed, however, we puff out our chests and boast of our vast skill, cunning and prowess in subduing our foe – who, by the way, has a brain the size of a sultana.

The maxim that 10 per cent of fishos catch 90 per cent of the fish is unfortunately true. This is particularly unfortunate if you're among the hapless 90 per cent – where The Tinny Twosome undeniably reside.

When perusing the stellar catches proudly paraded by the other 10 per cent in angling magazines and TV fishing shows, we are like gawky teenage girls gazing enviously at supermodels gracing the pages of fashion glossies, waiting and yearning and hoping to bloom into similarly magnificent creatures – but we know in our hearts that we never will.

It doesn't stop us having a crack though, does it? The defining traits that denote the species *fisho ordinarus* are an oft-misplaced but bottomless well of optimism – coupled with an insatiable gluttony for punishment.

Why else would we continually bake our brains in sweltering conditions that would force the maddest of dogs and Englishmen to seek shade and shelter; or brave horizontal sheets of tempest-driven rain and windchill factors that would have Mawson whimpering for a hot Milo and Mummy?

We endure estuarine assaults by biting insects capable of sending the most balanced person insane with itch and bite. We smash through miles of rough seas that pound kidneys, backs and knees. Then we bash back through miles of bush track on return to dry land, destroying vehicle, trailer, bank balance and sometimes the will to live.

We continually risk spontaneous electric incineration by cavalierly waving long graphite conductors around in pyrotechnic, tropical storms. We abseil down sheer, precipitous cliff faces to take up perilous toeholds on surf-battered shelves of sea-polished rock.

We head out riding high on the giddying euphoria of raised hopes – only to return dirty, dishevelled, depressed and often drunk, with those same hopes resoundingly crushed and usually with little or nothing to show for our toil and suffering except an empty esky and fuel tank.

Would we do it all again the next day, though? Abso-bloody-lutely! Why? Because we love it! We in The Tinny look at it as a spiritual thing: fishos don't regard piscatorial pursuits as some form of tangible catch-and-release or catch-and-cook tally. It's more the act of collecting a succession of perfectly formed pebbles in order to pave the path to divine self-enlightenment – through fish.

We are a league of lay philosophers and great thinkers. The depth of our contemplation is evident in the many mantras displayed proudly on rear windows and tailgates across the land: 'I fish and I vote'; 'My other car is a boat'; 'Shut up and fish'; 'Born to fish, forced to work' and the simple central tenet of our very Zen existence here in The Tinny – 'I fish, therefore, I am.'

You might like to take a moment to allow that profound philosophical mission statement to resonate deep within the very core of your soul – before I drag your focus back to the purely practical, worldly task of outlining the literary mechanics of *Tales from The Tinny.*

It will be me, Robert Smith, who will pound away at the keyboard with two blunt forefingers to chronicle the creature that is, *Tales from The Tinny.* Ostensibly, this is due to Tim's claims that he couldn't be bothered with the writing caper (couldn't give a rat's arse were his exact words) and that he would much rather be fishing, playing with his motorbike or drinking beer. This may well be true, but his reluctance only serves to strengthen my growing suspicion that he is actually a functioning illiterate.

Get a Mullet Up Ya! the book, will run pretty much along the lines of *Tales from The Tinny* radio program: it will be unapologetically parochial, irreverent to the point of insufferable, and opinionated to the point of ignorance. I shall employ language that is sometimes quite offensive and often highly vernacular.

I will not shy away from confronting the controversial issues that are generally inappropriate topics for polite social discussion such as religion, politics and sex. I will try to paint a picture of *our*

Top End, which may not necessarily match the generally held and widely promoted postcard perceptions. I will bring you yarns of bravery and stupidity, tragedy and triumph, infantile idiocy and true Territory toughness.

When thrown together in the crucible of strained credulity, these disparate parts will mix and meld to form the curiously compelling amalgam that is, *Tales from The Tinny.*

So, without further ado, and in the nicest possible way of course –

Get a mullet up ya !

Introducing the snapping handbag

THIS IS A book about fishing. This is a book about the Territory. So how could I possibly get underway in any other way than to talk about crocs?

When you think of the Territory, you think of crocs. It's an instant and unavoidable mental association. Territorians simultaneously celebrate, venerate, demonise and most of all, commercialise, our large, leathery mascots. We have croc slippers, croc hats, croc oven mitts – even T-shirts supposedly ripped and bloodied in a croc attack.

There is a croc aquarium complex in the tourist strip of Mitchell Street where you can swim with crocs in the 'Cage of Death!'. There is a dedicated croc park on the outskirts of town that also boasts a smattering of other exotic animals, presumably only to act as food stock for the main attraction because, let's face it, who wants to see any other animal in the Top End?

There is bitter competition between 'Jumping Crocs' cruise tour rivals on the nearby Adelaide River where the stars of the show are encouraged to leap vertically out of the water (well over the gunwale height of any fishing boat) and grab a snack of manky, old battery hen from the end of a raised stick.

Our local newspaper headlines any story with a tenuous link to crocs and every Top End tourism brochure has a croc lurking menacingly somewhere on the margin. Wildlife-park staff nurse baby crocs with taped snouts in the mall during the dry season, allowing tourists to avail themselves of a five-buck cuddle and photo opportunity. Many of our roadside signs carry croc caricatures and the Northern Territory government even took out croc insurance for President Obama when he visited the Top End.

We are fair dinkum croc crazy! It used to be said that Australia rode on the sheep's back – well I reckon it would be fair enough to say that the Top End is carried on the back of the salty.

Before we go on, a bit of biological clarification is required. When we talk about crocs in the Top End, it is generally accepted we are referring to the mighty *Crocodylus porosus* – the saltwater or estuarine crocodile – not their smaller, more reserved cousin, the freshy or *Crocodylus johnsoni*.

The freshy has a narrower snout and doesn't grow anywhere near as big as the salty. Consequently, they have a much lower media profile.

Apart from size, the main difference between them is their temperament. A freshy may give you a nasty self-defensive chomp on the leg if it feels threatened, but a salty will tear your whole leg off at the hip for no particular reason at all.

The croc is an evolutionary masterpiece; a patient, stealthy, awesomely powerful predator that deserves its unchallenged position at the pinnacle of the Territory food chain.

It is the largest living reptile on the planet; growing to a size of over 6 m in length and 1000 kg in weight. It has the ability to approach a fully grown buffalo totally undetected, explode out of the water, grab it by the snout and drag it to its watery demise. Its immensely powerful jaws can easily crush the luckless bovine's skull.

Curiously enough, this devastating power is only available when closing, not opening its jaws. Just a few loops of duct tape will quite successfully clamp even a fairly sizeable salty's jaws shut. Putting yourself in a position to apply the duct tape, however, provides its own set of unique challenges.

Crocs are increasing in both number and size, and most worryingly, seem to be losing their wariness of human beings. This is quite understandable given today's real big boppers were only young 'uns when croc shooting was stopped in the early '70s. This is becoming a bit of a concern, particularly during mating season when things can get a bit hairy in the handbag world. During this time, the big, dominant males stake out their territory and see off numerous challenges from toey young bucks full of ticker and testosterone, looking to make a claim on the old fella's turf and womenfolk.

Speaking of the fairer sex, they are no slouches in the kill, maim and mutilate department themselves. Maternal aggression is also running at peak level during this time as they vigorously guard nesting sites. Their maternal instinct is strangely short-lived though. Once the hatchlings burst out of the egg and make their way to water, Mum couldn't care less what happens to them: 'You're on your own, you little buggers, don't expect me to hang around to kill and dismember for you!'

The number of big salties is definitely on the rise. The number of boats and fishos, many of whom are new to the Territory and croc-survival etiquette, is also increasing. Put these two population explosions into close proximity on the same waterways and there are bound to be incidents.

As I mentioned croc shooting stopped in the early '70s, legally, that is. Old timers will tell you stories about having bush picnics and letting the kids swim about in places like Yellow Water and the Daly. Generally, there'd be someone keeping half an eye on proceedings with a .303 close at hand, but big crocs had pretty much been shot out of popular waterholes by that time. Those that were around were painfully aware of the association between the two-legged monkeys carrying a big stick that goes bang and Mummy and Daddy going belly up in the billabong in a spreading plume of blood.

Those days are long gone. Crocs are certainly not in any peril of dying out these days, as far as I can see. The old adage that even if you can't see the croc, rest assured he can see you, is an invaluable *aide-memoire* in avoiding the famed 'death roll' from the punter's perspective.

It can be astounding just how many crocs a relatively small waterway can host. A cautious walk down to the water's edge at night can prove this beyond doubt. Cast around the waterline is the mullet haircut, which has its inherent comical connotations of bogandom. It can be employed as a term of good-natured abuse, as in, 'Get out of it, ya mullet!'

One of my mates refers to me exclusively as mullet guts and I use an email address that includes mullet boy in the script. It also works magnificently as a phallic euphemism: 'So then he just walks up to their table, flops out his mullet and drops it in their jug. Classic!'

My favourite application, however, is as part of a phrase that I acquired in high school on Queensland's Sunshine Coast. It has never left me: 'Get a mullet up ya!'

The genesis of 'Get a mullet up ya' is lost in the mists of adolescent memory. I don't remember how or when it first came to prominence in my personal lexicon. It may have been a saying that was generated from within my group of mates; it may have been in wide use in the region and we just adopted it with gusto. I'm not sure. What I do know is that I have been tireless in my efforts to promulgate its widespread use and promote its virtues as one of the most utilitarian phrases in Australian vernacular language.

While not actually implying that you should insert a fish up your back passage, that mental picture can never be totally isolated from the phrase itself. I believe this factor lends the saying its undeniable visceral potency. It operates as a term of good-natured abuse; as a greeting or as a final, terse retort in a verbal joust: 'Aah, get a mullet up ya!' It provides something marvellously inappropriate to shout out in public at an equally inappropriate moment.

If you randomly insert 'Get a mullet up ya!' into a conversation in which you have found yourself to be totally out of your intellectual depth, it will garner a shocked chuckle from the gathering and cover for the fact that you are stuck for anything remotely relevant to contribute. You can then give a knowing wink as if alluding to some inferred significance hidden in the remark and walk away leaving your audience somewhat confused – but with the impression that you may possibly be an eccentric genius.

It can also work as an aural identifier, a tribal marker or in a challenge-and-respond capacity. For example, I can see a boat full of blokes trolling down the opposite bank of a big river. I think I might recognise them; they think they might recognise me. The usual combination of large hats, sunglasses and long sleeve baggy shirts obscures personal features and makes positive identification difficult. If they were to yell through cupped hands, 'Save the whales!' or 'I fish and I vote,' or even, 'My kitchen rules!' I would studiously ignore them or possibly even afford them a two-finger salute.

However, should they regale me with a rousing, 'Get a mullet up ya!', I would instantly wave them over to raft up for a celebratory ale. Even if they proved not to be mates of mine beforehand, they would be before very long.

When Tim and I were first developing the framework for what was to become *Tales from The Tinny*, 'Get a mullet up ya!' was the working title of the program. Unfortunately, ABC marketing and managerial forces were significantly underwhelmed by the concept and put an absolute veto on the proposition. No amount of pitching creative scenarios and applications, of cajoling or crawling or chucking screamingly spectacular tantrums would see the edict turned around. No sense of adventure, management.

'Get a mullet up ya!' has, however, become something of an unofficial catch phrase of The Tinny. Across crowds at the bustling Darwin markets, riding my bike on the Nightcliff foreshore, in shopping-centre and boat-ramp car parks, I am often accosted by someone bellowing, 'Oi, get a mullet up ya!'

I have even had a couple of instances of parents sending their small children over to randomly tug on my shirt to gain my attention before delivering, 'Get a mullet up ya!' In echoes of one of the scenarios outlined above, I have been greeted on the water with the same by boatloads of blokes who somehow recognise my lanky frame or dulcet vocal tones.

Tim and I consider the fact that total strangers feel comfortable hurling program-related abuse at us, loudly, and in public places, a satisfying key performance indicator that The Tinny is hitting the right note with the audience. You save your best abuse for your closest of mates, after all.

It is just a little disturbing that people have penetrated what we perceive to be the protective cloak of anonymity that radio provides, but at least we haven't had rocks thrown at us – yet.

Ode to the mullet

As mentioned previously, my fixation with *Mugil cephalus* borders on the unnatural. I was even moved to wax lyrical about my favourite baitfish and linguistic muse and producing a musically accompanied piece of 'performance poetry' for The Tinny. It goes a little something like this …

Ode to the mullet

How do I love thee?
Let me count thy scales,
Noble, schooling, estuarine creature.
Thou art a fine tasty morsel,
From pectoral to dorsal.
'Tis no wonder mobs queue up to eat ya.

I love thee to the depth and breadth,
That cast net and sounder dost reach.

I love thy gift of self-sacrifice,
Made from back eddy, creek bank and beach.

I love thee freely, or if not totally free,
As fair trade for beer or maybe ice.
I love thee purely – you, no other;
No surrogate will suffice.

I love thee with raging desire so keen,
Cold buckets of water shall nay dull it.
You are my mate, my bait,
And as I stick a hook up thy date,
I thank the almighty for you –
Faithful mullet.

Rule number one

When I first came to the Territory some eighteen years ago, I was desperate to get a line in the water. My long-held perception of the Top End as the fabled, promised land of bountiful angling had me champing at the bit. I received calls almost daily from fishing mates back home asking me feverishly, 'Have ya been fishin' yet?'

It took me a couple of weeks to drop enough sledgehammer hints around the office (damn work and its interfering demands on your time!), but finally a bloke relented and offered to take me out in one of the harbour arms that weekend.

The days dragged interminably towards Saturday as my excitement escalated into an all-consuming, sleep-depriving, lather of anticipation. My wife was quite used to these manic, pre-fishing-trip episodes from much experience 'down south' (as we had learned was the appropriate terminology for any place in Australia that wasn't the Top End). This presentation, however, was so extreme that she was not quite sure how to respond – with scorn, sarcasm and ridicule in an attempt to snap me out of my state; or with pity and a genuine concern for my mental welfare.

I was exhibiting a total lack of engagement in conversation and an inability to effectively focus on immediate tasks. When I wasn't nervously fidgeting or restlessly wandering, I would stare wistfully off into the distance, oblivious to all around me.

By Thursday evening, my wife gave up all attempts to communicate with me or seek any form of cogent response. She had decided that simply ignoring me was the best option, navigating around me in the house like you would a drifting sea container on the ocean.

Finally the weekend was upon us! My mate had said he would swing by with boat in tow to pick me up, 'Nice and early, alright?' The 'nice and early' was an irrelevant stipulation in this instance of course – I had been wide-awake and on a hair trigger since late the previous evening.

The sound of a diesel vehicle approaching in the distance disturbed the suburban silence in the grey light of pre-dawn. Soon I was able to discern that the motor was accompanied by a symphony of squeaks, clunks and rattles that indicated the presence of a boat on a trailer. The noise amplified as it got closer, the flash of headlights lit up the house on the corner of our street and finally the chariot of destiny materialised around the bend.

In a pathetic show of 'gammin' nonchalance, I waved lackadaisically as the headlights caught me in their glare to indicate our location. The rig pulled to a halt outside our driveway and my new mate rolled down the driver's window. I ambled across and leaned casually on the door pillar of the 4WD.

'Good day for it, mate,' I said, striving for laid-back but achieving contrived.

It was an excruciatingly difficult exercise in self-control. Internally I was red-lining on excitement, while outwardly I was desperately trying to maintain an impenetrable facade of cool, calm composure.

I loaded my rods and tackle box into the boat, tucker and drinks into the esky and we were ready to go. My wife waved from the footpath in her sarong, probably consumed with an overwhelming sense of relief as my new mate and I disappeared around the corner.

The target for the day's mission was Middle Arm. We chatted as we drove the 50 km or so to the bush ramp. Well, I chatted endlessly while he just nodded and grunted, still half asleep. On arrival, we launched his little 12-foot tinny, and while I held the nose, the skipper got aboard and negotiated his way through the assortment of eskies and rods and other clutter to assume his regulation position on the rear bench seat.

After a pull or two, the motor coughed lumpily to life and settled into a steadyish rhythm. I pushed us off into the current and clambered aboard in a single balletic motion, breathing a quiet sigh of relief as I did. The last thing I wanted to do was go arse up and become a tangle of legs and arms in the bottom of the boat, surrounded by upturned tackle boxes and in need of an emergency lure extraction before we even got underway.

Such acts of overeager clumsiness are not outside my performance repertoire and I had been dreading leaving such a lasting first impression on my new mate. That hurdle had now been successfully negotiated, and I took it as a good omen for the rest of the trip.

The skipper backed us further into the current out of harm's way, knocked the chugging two-stroke into neutral, turned and addressed me in a fairly formal tone.

'Right. There's only a coupla rules aboard my tinny, mate.'

I paid dutiful attention as he held one grease-stained finger up in front of my face.

'Rule number one: Stay in the boat at all times.'

A second finger joined the first, this one not quite as greasy as the first, but still bleeding slightly from a superficial cut suffered somewhere in the launch process.

'Rule number two: Do nothing that may in any way jeopardise the successful observation of Rule number one.'

I was getting the hang of this now, so the appearance of a comparatively unremarkable third finger came as no great surprise.

'Rule number three: Refer back to Rule number one. You got that?'

I did get that. I don't recall whether we even caught anything on that incredibly eagerly anticipated maiden Territory voyage, though I suspect not. I'm quite sure I would remember had we done so. I do remember that sage advice, however, and to this day, I recite it almost verbatim to newbies coming aboard my boat, often using the dramatic impact that the three greasy fingers method adds to the presentation.

It is very basic advice and may seem quite obvious, but when you have punters on your boat fresh from down south, dizzy with excitement and nervous energy – or maybe with a few cans on board already – it pays to reinforce it.

The reasons are myriad. Crocs, sharks, rays, stingers, swift currents, submerged snags and tropical infections – all of which have the ability to take a leg, or worse, if you don't respect them. *Inside* the tinny is definitely the preferable place to keep your posterior planted.

Tales from *out* of the tinny

SOMETIMES HOWEVER THE BEST laid plans of mullet and men can come horribly unstuck. Strictly self-imposed rules can be inadvertently broken, even by the most careful and experienced. I've got a few tales from *out* of the tinny to sprinkle through the book. Here's the first.

Mal and his mate Mick were fishing off Charles Point in Darwin Harbour one sticky build-up day in November. Charles Point is the site of a lighthouse, and marks the western extremity of Darwin Harbour. About 25 km as the crow flies from the city itself, the waters around Charles Point contain many shoals, holes and bommies that are a favoured hunting ground for jewies and snapper.

The boys had been doing OK with the jewies over recent times on a couple of their favourite waypoints, so they had high hopes of a repeat performance on this outing. There was a perfect harbour glass-off in effect, the tides were ideal and being mid week, they had the place to themselves. Despite the textbook conditions, however, not a scale had been raised the whole morning. They had tried a number of previously productive spots in the general area and couldn't seem to give bait away.

The writing appeared to be on the wall and it was getting pretty close to fat sheila yodelling time when Mal noticed some splashing out to the north, right out towards the horizon.

Splashing on a flat ocean always galvanises a fisho's attention because it generally flags some sort of pelagic action – mackerel, trevally or tuna smashing up baitfish on the surface. Something about this disturbance wasn't quite right, though. It didn't look like pelagics or dolphins or turtles. It was nothing recognisable at all, in fact. The fish weren't cooperating in the slightest, so the boys decided to pull anchor and head over for a look before making their way back into the harbour.

As they neared the mysterious splashing, Mal said, 'I reckon it's a bloke swimming!'

Mick scoffed. 'Where the bloody hell's someone gonna swim from out here?'

But as they got even closer, it became apparent it was indeed a bloke having a swim! They couldn't believe their eyes. Pulling the tinny alongside the intrepid adventurer, they asked, 'You alright, mate?'

Now it may seem like a rhetorical question – surely someone floundering around in the open ocean 20 km from the nearest civilisation is, by definition, in trouble. You just never know in the Territory, though. It always pays to ask.

'Well, no I'm not actually,' the bloke replied after a short pause, as if he had taken a moment to consider whether or not he was indeed in strife.

‘Do you want us to pull you in?’ offered Mal.

‘Ah, yeah, that’d be good. Ta.’

Between them, Mal and Mick skull-dragged the near-exhausted heap of human flotsam into the tinny. After an appropriate pause to let the poor bugger wheeze, cough, have a bit of a saltwater whommy and get himself back together, they got around to asking him the obvious question, ‘What the bloody hell were ya doin’?’

Flotsam told them he had been anchored up on a bommy (a rocky outcrop or ‘lump’ on the sea floor) in his own boat further out to sea with plans to pull an overnighter. He had been fishing for a while with no results (which made Mal and Mick feel a little better) when the build-up heat, in combination with an unspecified number of beers, had caused a synaptic misfire that led him to conclude it would be a great idea to dive overboard for a quick dip and cool down.

Acting quickly on this inspired impulse and without so much as a millisecond of analytical assessment of the possible consequences, he dived headlong over the side. When he resurfaced from his duck dive, he felt refreshed and revitalised from the cooling ocean waters. His enjoyment of the invigorating briny quickly turned to concern, though, as he realised the current had him firmly in its grip.

He struck out in a vigorous freestyle, attempting to regain the safety of his transom but there was no chance. He couldn’t swim anywhere near fast enough to overcome the tidal run. His helpless drift on the prevailing current, roughly in the direction of Shoal Bay, was underway. This might have seen him attain land in maybe two or three days’ time, barring intervention by sea creature or drowning, so as you can imagine, he was most grateful that the boys had intervened.

Mick and Mal (this yarn's starting to sound like a Leyland Brothers adventure, isn't it?) pointed their tinny with its recovering human cargo aboard into the current and backtracked along what they estimated to be the drift line. Sure enough, three or four miles away, they saw a shape starting to form on the horizon. They eventually pulled alongside the abandoned 'ghost tinny', which was happily bobbing away at anchor.

Flotsam had sobered up considerably by this stage. This tends to happen when your life has flashed before your eyes, apparently. He jumped back aboard his own boat and thanked the boys, indicating he might not actually proceed with his original plan of an overnight jewie vigil given his recent excitement. Mick and Mal motored off as Flotsam organised himself and made preparations to pull anchor, and that was the last they saw of him.

Circumstance can be an amazing thing. *If* the wind had been up the slightest degree, there would have been surface chop and Mal wouldn't have spotted the bloke splashing on the horizon. *If* the fish had been biting, their attention wouldn't have wandered to the point where you begin staring off into the distance. *If* they hadn't gone fishing that day, there was not another boat for many miles around. Flotsam was a very lucky boy.

The burning question that occupied Mal and Mick's retrospective discussions over a few beers in subsequent weeks though was, 'Do you reckon he told anyone what happened when he got home?'

We don't reckon he did. Would you have?

I refer you back to Rule number one.

Seasons

ALL LIFE IN the Top End is dominated, shaped and determined by the weather. Nowhere else in Australia are lifestyles, leisure activities, dress standards, architecture and overall attitude so inextricably intertwined into the endless ebb and flow of the seasonal cycle.

We wear our weather as a badge of honour, just another demonstration of our Territory toughness. Nowhere else has heat and humidity that even approaches the oppressive ferocity of our build-up. Nowhere else can match the aural, visual and visceral impact of our apocalyptic electrical storms. Nowhere else is subjected to the deafening downpours of our magnificent monsoons. No nirvana can hope to compare with the balmy tropical paradise that is the Top End in the dry.

Conditions in the tropics can be punishing and extreme, but they reckon if it doesn't kill you, it can only make you stronger. There is a fairly widely held school of thought that there are two types of people in this regard: those who can hack it, and those who don't stand a chance.

Darwin is, and always has been, a very transient town. Having been administered by the Federal Government or South Australia for large parts of its history, there has always been a roundabout of public servants, bank workers and corporate juniors doing their time in the backwater outpost of the Northern Territory. More recently, the major presence of defence personnel in the region has seen another regular rotation of new Top Enders.

Those who can hack it generally embrace the extremes with an exuberant passion almost instantly. They are quite happy at the prospect of spending their designated term in this new, wild and exciting frontier. These terms are sometimes designated by employers and may be just a matter of months. Other times, it can just be a nominal period of time pencilled in before arrival: 'We reckon we'll give it two years and then head back/move on.'

Often by the time these nominal terms expire though, the 'hack it' mob have developed a very strong emotional attachment to this strange and wonderful place. This development was not part of the original plan. The sense of 'we like it here' has solidified into an attitude of, 'we can't leave'. I wish I had a dollar for the number of times I've heard variations on the theme of, 'I got transferred up here for a three-month stint – that was 32 years ago.'

On the other hand, the 'don't stand a chance' mob stand out like dogs' proverbials from day one. They make little attempt to dress for the climate and are often visibly and volubly appalled by the ruling, ultra-casual dress etiquette. They are determined to maintain the mode and standard of acceptable presentation from whence they came.

They are mortified by their own newly developed propensity to perspire, and are utterly sickened and repulsed by the sweaty, smelly bodies of the loathsome local creatures that populate this malodorous tropical hell. 'Can't they smell themselves? They don't seem to care!'

They live in climatic denial and attempt to maintain a bubble-to-bubble existence, hopping quickly from air-conditioned house or apartment to air-conditioned vehicle to air-conditioned shop or office with minimal possible exposure to the horrendous elements. When they are forced to endure the outside, they continually complain about the heat and humidity, their indignant cheeks flushed with atmospheric distress.

The manyana timeframe that the Territory works on drives them to the brink of frustrated insanity. They will stamp their feet petulantly, complain and bang desks as they demand satisfactory service, only to be greeted with wry grins of amusement. 'You must be new to the Territory, eh?'

Now there is a fine line of demarcation here that must be explained. Whingeing about the weather is a favourite and widely practised local pastime. We enjoy it, we do it really well, and we do it a lot. Whining about the weather is an altogether different, and rather tiresome, kettle of fish. The difference between a whinge and a whine is the subtext, nuance and hidden inferences contained therein.

When the newly introduced 'hack it' mob and the longer-term, well-established Top End locals say something along the lines of, 'God, the weather's filthy. It's absolutely disgusting out there!'

what they really mean is, 'Isn't it impressive, the extreme levels of discomfort that our fabulous Top End has the ability to throw at us, and aren't we privileged to be able to experience it.'

Whereas, when the 'don't stand a chance' mob say the same thing, they actually mean, 'I don't think I can survive another day in this festering hell hole. I can't believe I allowed myself to be talked into coming here and the only faint glimmer of hope I retain in my miserable existence is the prospect of boarding the air-conditioned jet that will free me from this purgatory. A pox on you, Top End!'

Can you see the difference? The 'don't stand a chance' mob don't last long and don't belong when they are here anyway, so let us not concern ourselves with them any further and return our focus to local conditions.

It is a fact that we have the most predictable weather patterns in the country. There is a certain comfort in not having to endure a wide variation in climatic conditions from month to month – or even in the same day as is often experienced by many of our southern cousins.

The concept of Melbourne's much-vaunted four seasons in one day is the stuff of waking nightmares for most Top Enders. We operate in a fairly narrow, environmental envelope – our daytime maximums generally only range from 30 to 35° Celsius year round – and we become very intolerant of change.

These tight temperature parameters have quite a few advantages, the most apparent being the ability to dress in one style of clothing all year round. Shorts, T-shirts, singlets, sarongs and thongs are de rigueur and will suffice for all but the most formal of occasions.

You may come across a pub or club in the Top End that bears a sign out the front stating that dress codes apply after six. This is simply there to remind the more obtuse that they may be required to actually wear some – clothes, that is.

Not having to tool up with different wardrobes for different seasonal conditions saves a considerable amount of money, particularly if you follow the long-established Top End tradition of periodically buying a couple of years' worth of outfits in one decisive swoop on the sweatshops of Bali or some other South-East Asian holiday destination.

Humidity is the greatest variant in our climate and the one that sends player-comfort levels off the scales in the negative direction. Even so, there is a reassuring predictability in its incremental increase and gradual decline.

There are very few surprises or unexpected climatic events in the Top End. You can actually produce your very own, reliably accurate, daily weather forecast, simply by having an awareness of what month it is. Planning outdoor dry-season events years in advance is an absolute cinch. You can confidently rely on a '32° and fine' report from early May through to late August.

Our poor Bureau of Meteorology (otherwise known as BOM) staff bear the brunt of many standing jokes. Most of these are generated from the widely held belief that they just turn up to work to soak up the free air-con, play office quoits and darts, or do online shopping and play World of Warcraft.

According to this urban myth, the duty forecaster rostered for the day strikes a blow for public-service productivity by sending out the '32° and fine' or '35° and a late thunderstorm' notification, without so much as a look out the window, let alone a licked-finger lifted aloft.

This is a baseless, ill-informed and unfair denigration of our fine and industrious BOM staff. I can provide a first-hand, eye-witness account confirming that the duty forecaster does in fact look out the window from time to time, though I think the finger-licking trick has long gone out of fashion.

In all truth though, the BOM mob really do earn their pay, particularly in the cyclone season. These big scary whirligigs provide the sting in the tail and random x-factor to our existence in the tropics. Each cyclone season two or three threaten the Top End coastline. Should they happen to inconveniently head in your direction, this demands the shuttering up and locking down of your house.

Though both important and necessary for the protection of life and property, it is at the same time a major pain in the ring – particularly if you have a couple of episodes in the one season. Tracy looms large in everyone's consciousness here, particularly those who lived through her. Every year there is that niggling concern, 'Is this the year of the big one?'

Summer, winter, autumn and spring are terms that mean nothing to us in the Top End. They are a foreign notion from a faraway place, much like the rest of Australia views the concept of a white Christmas. We know what it's about, we've seen it on TV – but it has absolutely no relevance to us whatsoever.

The Yolngu people of Arnhem Land work on a calendar containing six seasons delineated by distinct changes in local flora, animal activity and weather patterns. Many whitefellas strip it back to plain old wet and dry, but there are a number of seasonal subsets closely related to the Yolngu calendar contained in that broad simplification.

The life cycle and behaviour of fish, particularly the iconic barramundi, is also driven by the seasonal oscillation. Access to rivers, billabongs and whole regions of the Territory is dictated by rainfall. The conditions on the harbours and ocean are dependent on the weather, and the species you might target also change with the season.

Given these fairly obvious statements, it should probably come as no surprise that fishos discuss the weather even more excessively than normal Top Enders. Having said that, I'm yet to meet a 'normal' Top Ender.

It is impossible to gain a true perspective of our world up here without an understanding of the great climatic cycle that drives it. Though there is no real substitute for actually living it, bear with me as I attempt to evoke the sights, sounds and smells of our individual Top End seasons.

Let me start with my personal favourite, the wet.

The wet

THE BOM DECLARES the wet to be underway as of the first of October every year. They require a regimented approach to seasonal delineation in order to facilitate the gathering of accurate comparative data, hence the hard and fast line in the sand. In reality, variations from year to year mean that the fair dinkum start of the wet moves all around the latter stages of the calendar. I personally don't consider the wet to be underway until we have had our first burst of good monsoonal weather.

When that first burst of magnificent big-M weather hits, you can almost hear a collective sigh of relief across the Top End. By that stage we have generally suffered through the oppressive worst of the build-up and are clamouring for deliverance from the seemingly endless succession of punishingly hot and humid days.

Build-up storms can bring fleeting relief and a degree of rain, but they are generally fast-moving and isolated. Often they only serve the frustrating function of increasing the humidity and level of discomfort in the wake of their passing.

Monsoonal rain, in contrast, digs in for the long haul. When the Top End is in the grip of an active monsoonal trough, the rain alternates between torrential and heavy, with an occasional window of drizzle or no rain at all thrown in just to mix it up. The temperature plummets. While the rest of Australia may be gripped in a sweltering heatwave, flocking to the beaches and putting the national electricity grid under terminal strain from air-con load, we are often enjoying our coolest days of the year.

If you look on a weather map and see Darwin with a forecast max of 29°, you can bet your house on the fact that it is piss-istently precipitating. The accompanying minimum is likely to be about 27° as well – a nice narrow window to operate in!

During the monsoon, the countryside undergoes a stunning metamorphosis. Roadside bush that was dirt, dust and rock transforms into an explosively contrasting palette of vibrant green new growth set against the stark red of freshly washed ochre dirt. Spear grass jungles seem to instantly shoot up and soon tower over the countryside to heights of about 6 feet.

Suburban parklands that were dry, brown dust bowls only days before are reborn as lush, verdant carpets of green. Home gardens leap out of the blocks like they have been shot full of vegie steroids. Amazing spurts of growth appear to be happening before your very eyes.

Lawn mowing is an onerous, torturous, mind-numbingly futile chore. I banished this vile curse from my life many years ago by replacing *all* lawn with either garden, paving, concrete or pebbles. Those poor suffering wretches who persist with their grassy fetish find themselves enslaved to their foolish folly. You may only have mown your lawn once in the previous six months, but in the wet, you suddenly find yourself mowing it every six hours.

There's a line contained in one of those joke lists that gets emailed around that says, 'You know you're a Territorian when you mow your lawn and find a troop carrier.' Though quite a comical image, this is not out of the realms of possibility.

The first burst of monsoon also signals the commencement of an extraordinary amphibian display of wanton sexual abandon. Frogs launch into an orgy of – not to put too fine a point on it – orgying! The lustful cries that resonate around the suburbs are absolutely deafening as the frog orgy begins.

The Smith household is designed very much along troppo architectural principles which maximise airflow and minimise reliance on air-cons. We therefore have no insect screens or solid windows and doors as such, just artistically rendered wrought iron. This generates a lovely indoor/outdoor feel and provides an effective barrier for keeping unwanted human visitors out – but presents no impediment whatsoever to frogs gaining access. Consequently, every vase, jar and plant pot in our house provides a convenient home in which a green tree frog will happily reside.

Sometimes, when suitable accommodation is at a premium, you will find two, three or more living cheek by jowl in the same squat. Frogs choose these receptacles because of their resonant sound amplification properties, and when the time comes to advertise for love, our living room becomes nigh-on uninhabitable. The cacophony is deafening. Forget any plan you might have had to watch TV or a video on a cosy rainy night. The sound level required from our stereo to overcome the amphibian symphony would be sufficient to puncture eardrums and unsettle the foundations of our house.

The pool is also a favoured destination for a bit of froggy leg-over. I have to routinely patrol the perimeter with a scoop net to evict loads of lust-addled interlopers piggybacking (or froggybacking?) in the pool.

During protracted monsoonal bursts, I need to backwash periodically to avoid the pool overflowing. First though, I must check the skimmer box because it seems to be sex pad central for hot, wet, froggy love. On one record-breaking occasion, I had to rescue fourteen frogs that were spinning endlessly round and round in the suction-induced vortex. They were coupled in pairs and threesomes and bizarre daisy chain–type configurations. It was like a Swedish hot-tub scene from a '70s porno flick!

The next step in the monsoonal progression is the mould phase. *Everything* goes mouldy. Leather items are often the first and most spectacular specimens to bloom. A sheen of grey–green fungal dusting will appear on boots, belts and bags. Next, the walls begin to follow suit and before you can say penicillin, it's on for young and old – or fuzz and mould? Benches, clothes, car seats, furniture – the whole world starts to go fuzzy. If you oversleep or spend protracted periods of time in front of a computer, you may well wake up in a blue–grey bloom yourself.

The whole world starts to take on the all-pervasive aroma of dankness, must and mildew. Because humidity constantly lingers around the 100 per cent mark, the bath towel you pull fresh out of the linen cupboard in November never really dries until about April.

All clothes are still slightly damp when you take them off the line, or whichever undercover spot you have used to drape your washing over in the forlorn hope that it will dry. Many people's dwellings take on the appearance of a Chinese laundry over the wet with sarongs, knickers and singlets draped over chair backs, door handles or even Balinese statuettes. Then, after storing them for a while in a dank, humid cupboard, your nice, clean clothes will often provide an olfactory surprise when you next pull them over your head.

There are definite social benefits to the onset of the wet, however. Rates of murder, road rage, domestic violence and episodes of hysterical public nudity plummet from their annual peaks attained during the build-up. A perceived slight or mild disagreement that a month before may well have degenerated into a tooth-and-nail punch-up may now just result in an affable, 'No worries, mate, it's sweet.'

Also, the wet is the only time when Top Enders can truly claim total dominion over their own territory. There is the total absence of visiting relatives, and only a sprinkling of hardcore tourists, southerners, foreigners and other annoyances.

The roads are often cut so you can't go anywhere. It's too wet to garden or do other outside work. The monsoon usually sets in somewhere around the Christmas/New Year/school holiday period, so it tends to reinforce the go-slow seasonal mode of operation that is already in full, inactive swing in the Territory. It's the perfect opportunity to relax, watch some cricket, and take some quality time to smell the mould!

As far as fishing goes, the peak of the monsoon is pretty much maintenance-and-preparation time. You service your reels and repack them with new line if necessary. Attend to those little jobs on the boat that have been annoying you all build-up, maybe even re-treble your lures.

Another important job for the fisho during the house-bound months is to endlessly discuss and deliberate on the prospects for the coming run-off, and formulate plans to get among the 'Metreys' – the revered metre-long barramundi that are caught prolifically at that time of year … if you are good enough.

The barramundi meanwhile are taking their lead from both the frogs and the fishos in their monsoonal activities. That is, they are going at the spawning caper much like their amphibian counterparts in the Swedish hot tub, and waiting with great anticipation for the run-off, just like their main predator.

In the ocean, the fish are obviously doing their thing, but the weather conditions make getting at them difficult and unproductive. The harbours are very patchy because the large amount of fresh water diluting the salt sends everyone off the chew.

One unique fishing opportunity does present itself at this time of year, however, culvert fishing. As the floodplains fill and begin to envelop large parts of the landscape, stormwater drains, inland bridges and flooded roads that may be arid gullies during the dry suddenly become viable barramundi spots as the fish push up to the extreme reaches of any waterway.

As the season progresses, the monsoon trough goes through inactive phases, and sometimes moves north over South-East Asia. This leaves us periods of relatively fine weather, and sometimes, small windows of opportunity for mini run-offs in the big rivers. During these lulls in rainfall, the water may start running back off the floodplains. Short, sharp, ferocious periods of barramundi activity can occur in these times – but you really have to be Johnny on the spot.

As the gaps between active monsoonal events lengthen, we move towards the end of the wet-season cycle. Just when you thought you were about to go stark-raving mad with mould and land-locked cabin fever, the season turns and the weather transitions from full-blooded monsoonal back to a pattern of more discrete storm activity. Big thumping storms the Yolngu people of Arnhem Land know as knock 'em downs – due to their propensity to flatten the now-drying spear grass of the Top End savannah – become the order of the day. The player-comfort meter begins to return to the very unattractive section of the dial with conditions much like build-up. Consequently, some people call this part of the year build-down.

The decrease in frequency and then the departure of the knock 'em downs signals the end of the wet, as such, but heralds the much-anticipated arrival of the red-letter, gilt-edged, absolute zenith of the barra fishing calendar ... the run-off!

Suburban slappers

You've got to be prepared to travel some distance to chase fish in the Territory – it's a *big* place. Most Top End fishos would think nothing of a day trip that involves driving a couple of hundred kilometres – a fair proportion of which would be over corrugated dirt track – to get to a remote boat ramp. There we launch the tinny and embark on another significant leg of the journey by boat in order to arrive at the final fishy destination. Then after the actual fishing is done, the whole arduous trip is undertaken in reverse on the homeward journey.

All these miles and effort are often undertaken purely on the strength of a vague rumour that the particular spot in question is 'going off'. It makes for a very big day at the office, particularly if you come home vanquished instead of victorious – the bruises, the sunburn and windburn, the aching muscles, fatigue and dehydration all seem that more pronounced when there's nothing in the esky to show for your trouble and there's a void in your wallet from the fossil fuel you've burned.

Sometimes in life, however, we complicate things unnecessarily. Great and unexpected rewards can often be found much closer to home – ridiculously close in this instance.

Anthony Holehouse is an aircraft engineer who works at Darwin Airport on a four-day-on, four-day-off cycle – the perfect roster for a keen fisho. It allows him to avoid the crowds of weekend warriors, plan frequent, extended trips, and fish on the most promising tides as opposed to the narrow window of opportunity that the Monday to Friday grind permits.

Anthony avoids the harbour and other current seasonal hotspots on weekends and public holidays, preferring to fish weekdays when 'most other buggers are at work'.

So it was that he found himself lounging around at home, rostered off but not fishing on an Australia Day public holiday. He tinkered around the house doing a few odd jobs without much enthusiasm and sat down to watch the cricket on telly for a while. By late afternoon, though, boredom had seriously set in.

He contemplated going for a random walk, but this seemed a bit pointless until he remembered seeing families and young kids fishing at a nearby suburban lagoon recently. A random walk with a rod in your hand was a different prospect!

Apparently you had a fair chance of putting your budding young angler onto a juvenile barramundi there and it provided an easily accessible venue to work the basic bugs out of the kiddie's technique in a safe, controlled environment close to home. Given that even small barra or 'rats' put on a bit of a show, especially on light gear, if you got your young tackers onto a fish, there was a very good chance that they would be irreversibly bitten by the bug. In a masterstroke of psychological and behavioural manipulation, the fisho parent could then channel the irresistible force of pester power to bring about their own desired outcomes. That is, increased fishing opportunities. Win! At the same time, the child thinks that they have had a victory. Win, win!

So, grabbing a flicking rod and some light gear, Anthony wandered the 500 m or so down to the lagoon, confident it would be a pleasant enough way to while away an hour or two.

Anthony lives in Palmerston, a satellite city just south of Darwin. A series of stepped lagoons were created in the midst of the suburbs of Gunn and Rosebery when they were first developed about 12 to 15 years previously. Conceived as a central landscaping feature of the developer's grand vision and gouged out around the course of an existing wet-season creek bed by bulldozer, they are very much an introduced feature. Sweeping lawn verges and cultivated native trees surround the shoreline, which is ringed by concrete paths for bike riding and dog-walking duties.

Rock retaining walls form the bank in places, concrete spillways and manufactured brooks mark the divide between different levels of lagoon and produce quaint little waterfalls that add a scenic and sonic contribution to the tableau. Strategically placed islands of quarried rock in the middle of the lagoon are ringed by introduced water lilies to promote a billabong feel. It's all very pretty, and an undeniably valuable asset to the suburban aesthetic – but at the same time, it is quite obviously man made.

Anthony went down to the lake carrying his flicking rod rigged with a 70 mm soft plastic lure and small 2/0 hook, and with no great expectation other than to pass a bit of time until dark forced him home. After a quick recce, he settled on a position that would be quite promising if encountered in the wild. There was a waterfall from the higher level of lake to his right, and a fairly thick belt of lily and weed surrounding the rocky shoreline of an island, a short cast away.

Fish, in general, and barramundi in particular, love features – snags, crags, rock bars, fallen logs. Anthony's targeted stretch of water held a particularly juicy bonus bit of 'feature' not often encountered in natural terrain: a half-submerged, partly rusted out shopping trolley protruded from the water just downstream from the waterfall.

There had been a few fairly heavy monsoonal showers earlier in the day and the spillway was running quite hard. It was around 6 pm and a light cloud cover remained from the earlier rain. Conditions were fairly gloomy as it approached sunset. Anthony reckoned he had an hour or so before dark.

The lilies looked a likely spot for a barra to be hiding so he started flicking over the back of them towards the rocky shoreline opposite, dragging the lure back through the mat of weed and lily stalks into the clear water closer to his bank. He had only been casting for a couple of minutes, but it was long enough for his thoughts to wander elsewhere. Suddenly, his mind was violently refocused on the job at hand as an almighty *BOOF!* shattered the suburban stillness.

Just as the 70-mm plastic cleared the lily bed, it had been absolutely clobbered by the monstrous inhalation of a bucket mouth – a *BIG* barramundi. Anthony spent a second or two in an attitude of slack-jawed disbelief as the slapper of a fish made a bolt for freedom through the lilies. The squeal of peeling line snapped him out of his stupor, and he cranked up the drag in an attempt to slow its progress.

Highly conscious of the single, rather flimsy barb on the hook that provided the tenuous attachment to what was obviously a sizeable fish, he concentrated on maintaining tension on the line. He could not afford to turn this battle into a skull-dragging tug of war; his gear was no match for this fish. He just persisted in tiring her out and making small retrievals between runs.

After a fair amount of this to-ing and fro-ing, he began to turn the big girl's head and finally felt he was gaining the upper hand in the battle. Luckily, the fish had made a run to weed and open water, not round the rocky corner of the island that would have signalled game over.

Eventually, he managed to get the fish in to the bank at his feet – whereupon the seriously under-gunned and heavily abraded leader gave way. Anthony's perception of events went into super slow-mo at this point (as happens in most action films these days at a moment of life-threatening circumstance). Conversely, Anthony's mind raced at the speed of light through alternative courses of action and associated consequences.

It was imperative that there was a photographic record of this creature. If he dared to try and spin this yarn without such incontrovertible evidence, he would be pilloried by all his mates and the wider fishing community as a liar, a buffoon and a tragic, drug-addled fantasist. He would be forced to bear the stigma of his perceived folly for decades.

'There's that dickhead who tried to tell everyone he caught a metrey out of Rosebery Lagoon.'

'Yeah. Sad bastard, isn't he?'

Without any tangible proof, he would be forced to keep the story to himself – a cracking yarn that would eat away corrosively at his insides over time if left untold.

His resolve hardened, his course of action became clear – and the slow-mo vision reverted to real time. With the speed of a striking cobra, Anthony leapt into the murky shallows and shoved a hand into the barra's cavernous bucket mouth as it sat almost immobile in the shallows, momentarily stunned into post-battle inertia. He grabbed it by the bottom jaw and hoisted it out onto the bank in one adrenaline-fuelled fluid motion.

There it was, flopping about on the grassy, manicured lawn. Not some fanciful hallucination, not some product of a feverishly overactive imagination – but flesh blood and scale and over a metre of it! Holding the fish aloft for the vindicating photo taken by an accommodating passer-by, arms still trembling with post-fight adrenal shakes, Anthony marvelled at the colour of the fish. While certainly not a true saltwater chromey, it was certainly no swamp dog as you might expect for a fish that had presumably spent its life in the very lagoon from which Anthony had pulled it.

After a few snaps were taken with the ever-handy mobile phone, and then a few more just in case, Anthony swam the slapper for a few minutes to get some water running over her gills and launched her back towards the depths of the lagoon.

As he watched the barra swim away, he congratulated himself on an eminently successful choice of activity to kill a bit of time. He wandered off home considerably pleased with himself and forwarded the photographic evidence of his afternoon's work to a few mates.

Predictably enough, word of this extraordinary catch spread around the fishing community like wildfire. The inevitable scoffs of disbelief and claims of outright fraud were largely quelled by the accompanying photo. We in The Tinny heard about it and lined Anthony up for a yarn on the show the next Saturday morning.

The legend of the Palmo Lagoon metrey gathered momentum. Anthony was still somewhat incredulous himself as we spoke to him on air.

'Mate I can't believe it. I was hoping to maybe catch a couple of 40-cm rats for a bit of fun and ended up getting walloped by that monster! I'm off to the newsagent to grab a swag of lotto tickets now!'

He hadn't caught a metrey up until that point in his career and we asked him if he considered that he was now on the board.

'Nah. That was a fish in a barrel. Not till I catch a wild fish – preferably a chromey.'

We like that attitude and congratulated him on his adoption of it.

Later on in the show, we got a text from a bloke calling himself simply Barry from Palmo. He remembered something about the lakes being stocked with fish and possibly red claw around the time of the big carnival hoo-ha that was held to celebrate the grand opening of the development. He did admit, however, that the details were a bit hazy because he was drunk at the time. You get that in the Territory.

We left the studios that morning shaking our heads and remarking on what an extraordinary yarn it was and how the Territory never ceased to surprise and amaze. The icing on the cake, however, was yet to come.

Anthony returned to the lagoon that Saturday arvo. He had absolutely no expectation of a repeat performance, but simply felt that the karmic balance was not correct. It was just not right to pull such an impressive fish from such an unlikely place with such a small investment of time and effort.

He believed that he owed the spot quite a few wasted flicks to re-establish some form of equilibrium in the effort-versus-reward equation. If left unaddressed, this imbalance might somehow come back to curse him on fair dinkum fishing ventures.

A belt of monsoonal rain had recently stopped, just as on that fateful Thursday. He took up the same possie, at the same spot, at the same time. He selected a soft plastic similar to the model that had done the damage previously, but slightly darker in colour in response to the water having dirtied up a bit. It exhibited a pronounced limp or stagger through the water on a test drag in the shallows (the result of having been left on a car dashboard for too long). He decided to look on this palsied action as a feature, or a point of difference, rather than a handicap, and persevered with this initial selection. After all, he wasn't going to catch anything anyway, was he?

His initial plan was to concentrate his efforts on the beautifully positioned fish-attracting device (or FAD) that had once been the property of Coles Supermarkets until it went down, down and stayed down. He flicked over towards the base of the vigorously flowing spillway and jinked the demented-looking rubber past the shopping trolley, only about a 20-foot cast and retrieve.

After about half a dozen flicks and with Anthony considering changing his target zone, the surface of the lagoon about 2 feet away from the trolley erupted into an immense maelstrom as a massive fish once again inhaled the small plastic lure with an almighty *BOOF!*

Contrary to the popular myth, lightning had indeed struck twice! 'You have got to be joking!' thought Andrew as this fish also bolted for the lilies. He cranked the drag up once more as an eerie sense of deja vu swept over him. The same fish, in the same spot, at the same time! Was this slapper a compulsive creature of habit, or just plain stupid? Had he unwittingly developed supernatural powers and evolved into not just a barra whisperer, but a metrey whisperer?

These burning questions would need to be contemplated in the fullness of time; the immediate task at hand was to deal with the horse bolting for the gate with some gusto at that very moment.

This fish sought and managed to attain the sanctuary of thick weed a number of times. Usually this is all over red rover in a fight as the hooked fish can use the weed to disengage from the hook or alternatively it becomes impossible to exert enough force to drag the fish through the thick vegetation without snapping your line.

Through a combination of good luck, good management and patience, Anthony was able to get the fish back out into open water. This presented a much more level playing field – and just as well, because he had calculated he had already exceeded his regulation quota of luck on this particular encounter.

Time passed, the hook, line and lure held, the fish began to tire and the tide turned once again in Anthony's favour. He began to make solid progress and before long, had the still-struggling fish flapping about in the shallows by the bank.

Once again, he was presented with the dilemma of what to do next. He had no landing net and the leader was nowhere near strong enough to drag the fish from the water. Holding the required tension on the line with the rod in one arm while bending down to try and grab and lift 12–15 kg of live fish is not the easiest exercise, either.

Luckily, at that moment, he noticed Jordan Smart, a local lad from a fisho family and a regular junior correspondent on The Tinny treadling by on his BMX. Anthony gave him a, 'Hoy, Jordan!' and beckoned him over. The young fella quickly assessed the situation upon arrival and without a moment's hesitation, leapt in to the lagoon to grab the impressive barra and drag it up onto dry land.

Once again, 1020 mm of *Lates calcarifer* lay flapping on the manicured lawns surrounding Rosebery Lagoon. As the whoops of victory, high fives and somewhat hysterical excitement abated, Anthony noticed something quite odd. He had understandably assumed he had just captured the same barra that obviously hadn't learnt any lesson from Thursday's adventure. After all, it was bizarre enough that there was one metrey in the lagoon – surely it couldn't hold another? As he looked closer though, he began to harbour doubts. Soon, these doubts were confirmed – this was not the same fish.

While exactly the same size at 1020, this barra was considerably cleaner than the first – it was almost chrome. Barra don't clean up that much in a couple of days, particularly in a muddy, fresh-water environment. The initial fish had a couple of distinctive splits in its tail webbing and this one didn't. Those things don't heal in a couple of days, either. He was suddenly convinced that this was indeed a different fish – which made the whole episode even more extraordinary!

The supplemental tale and another photo were posted on The Tinny website and what had already been a cause célèbre among the Darwin and Palmerston fishing community suddenly took on viral proportions. After initial scepticism from some sectors of the online community, the 'two fish' theory came to be accepted as fact. Close comparison of the photos revealed variations in body shape as well as differences in colour and the tail.

There were claims from some quarters that Anthony had single-handedly caused a surge in Palmerston real estate values and calls for the next suburb developed to be named in his honour. Others pushed for him to nominate and run in the mayoral race. The general consensus of online reaction can probably be summed up nicely with this contribution: 'Good on ya, mate! Classic. Ya gotta love the Territory!'

Meanwhile, Anthony fishes on in pursuit of his first 'real' metrey, an achievement which we in The Tinny are confident he will chalk up at some stage quite soon. Regardless of whether he does or not though, he has a cracking bit of barbecue banter he can roll out for the rest of his days. And who knows, maybe in Palmerston's future there will be a new suburban development centred on a system of interlinking lagoons that operate as a stocked impoundment for slapper barra.

It will surely go by the name of Holehouse Waters.

Wet work

DURING THE MONSOON, we get a lot of rain here in the Top End. I don't think I'm making any startling revelations there. As a result, it is quite a normal state of affairs for roads, both major and minor, to be cut repeatedly and sometimes protractedly over the duration of the wet season.

This is not generally an emergency situation or any great surprise. It is a regular and expected aspect of life in the Top End. The Arnhem, Stuart, Kakadu and Victoria highways are often cut at various stages through the wet, isolating small communities and major towns alike. Even Darwin is sometimes totally inaccessible by road from the rest of Australia, its arterial highways all cut simultaneously.

Light planes provide the only access to a lot of communities for the duration of the wet, and small tinnys and airboats come into their own as means of ferrying supplies and passengers across flooded stretches of road, sometimes kilometres wide.

This all means that most Territorians are familiar with wet work – traversing flooded stretches of road. Inevitably though, no matter how careful or experienced they are, occasionally people come unstuck.

Tourists are particularly prone to falling foul of flooded roads and crossings. The combination of inexperience, underestimating the force that fast-flowing water can exert, and the assumption that their hired 4WD is impervious to the forces of nature, brings many undone.

Being washed off flooded roads is highly dangerous at any time, but when you are being washed off a road into a crocodile-infested waterway, the dire nature of the predicament is significantly enhanced.

Cahills Crossing is the causeway across the East Alligator River providing access to Arnhem Land. It can generally be relied on for a number of wash-offs each year. Interestingly though, Cahills claims most of its victims away from the peaks of the wet-season river heights. This is because it is inaccessible at those times.

It is the tidal flow pushing right up the river from the ocean 80 km or so downstream, that surges up and over the crossing on large tides, that claims most victims on Cahills. Semitrailers, heavy work vehicles, 4WDs towing boats and 2WD sedans often end up perched precariously somewhere downstream. I have even been washed over the causeway in my little 13-foot tinny – but that's a tale for another time.

There are two boat ramps on the East Alligator – one upstream and one downstream of Cahill's Crossing. They provide access to the tidal and non-tidal (or, more accurately, less tidal) sections of this magnificent river.

A couple of years ago, a Euro tourist drove into the upstream car park and launch area in her hired 4WD. Seeing the concrete ramp disappearing into the water and assuming this was the crossing she had heard all about, she roared into the water. I'm not quite sure where she thought she was going to exit on the sheer bank opposite, but she never got an opportunity to find out as the vehicle promptly began disappearing into the depths of the river.

Luckily, she was able to overcome the initial shock, successfully extricate herself from the sinking 4WD, and make it back to dry land without drowning or being death-rolled by an opportunistic leathery bystander. She even managed to have the vehicle salvaged later. There was considerable uncharacteristic enthusiasm for the retrieval job by the local tow-truck crew and a prompt resolution of the situation, actually – primarily because the submerged vehicle was partially blocking the boat ramp: 'Bugger me, can't have that! Get it outta there!'

I suspect her car rental bill would have been significantly augmented by the whole exercise as well.

Variations on this story are stunningly common in the Top End.

For fishos, the time that most roads are in flood or are just starting to recede is also the time that they are itching to have a crack at the early run-off conditions in the big rivers. To illustrate the severity of this 'itch' and the lengths fishos will go to to scratch it, going the long way to the famous Shady Camp is a common mission at this stage of the wet.

Shady Camp is a barrage on the Mary River which minimises saltwater intrusion further into the system. There is an annual barra closure downstream from Shady from 1 October to 31 January.

'Shady' is usually about a 180–220-km drive from Darwin one-way. When the Arnhem highway is flooded between the Stuart highway and the Shady turn-off, you'll find many fishos are quite willing to drive via Pine Creek and Jabiru to access this run-off hotspot for a crack at the coastal creeks of the Mary. This blows the trip out to around 600 km each way. That's keen.

It is when the water depths begin to drop to around the metre mark that things start getting interesting. It is at this point that fishos start considering having a crack. We all exhibit widely varying degrees of bravado, prudence, skill, judgement and pure luck. The results are also widely varying.

There are a couple of yarns of fine, wet work that I'd like to spin you, but I'm going to start with a first-hand account …

Marrakai dunk

A COUPLE OF wet seasons ago, I was at a Saturday night BBQ having a few beers and discussing weighty matters of blokey significance. Nothing new or revolutionary there, but on this particular evening it was decided that a social road trip would be a smashing way to spend the next day.

We had been enjoying a fairly solid burst of monsoonal activity over the preceding week or two which resulted in most people's recreational activities being restricted to sitting around inside watching the mould grow, or sitting outside on covered decks watching the garden grow. This pretty much took care of the daylight hours. By evening, the ceaseless high-decibel serenade by frog symphonies would entertain well into the wee hours, with innumerable encores.

Though many Territorians (including this one) consider the monsoonal wet to be the most magnificent time of year in the Top End, you can tend to develop a sense of cabin fever if it continues unabated for too long.

The current deluge had eased off a bit during the day on Saturday, and the monsoon was predicted to remain inactive for the next day or two. This forecast, however unreliable, had galvanised the group to seize the opportunity and form a 4WD convoy for a pleasant Sunday social drive. Get out of town for a bit and take a jaunt down a bush track to see how the country was holding up under the annual flooding – what a good idea! Chuck a couple of flicking rods in the back in case we come across a likely looking roadside stream or culvert – excellent. Pack eskies full of nice nibbles, icy cold beers and a few champagnes – these last items for consumption by passengers only, of course – brilliant!

My vehicle was nominated alongside two others and the old Marrakai track linking the Stuart and Arnhem highways through the Adelaide River floodplain was elected as the path of choice. A very loose plan was formulated which basically involved heading as far down the track as we could before it inevitably disappeared into an expanse of wet-season floodplain. As always with trips like these, there would also be a keen eye kept out for any detours, distractions or alternative tracks that may present an amusing and interesting diversion.

And so it was the next morning, the motley convoy saddled up and headed out of town and down the track, with most a little dusty from the previous evening's deliberations (which had developed into quite thirsty work).

I probably should explain a bit of local terminology at this point before the tracks become a little confusing. To Territorians, 'The Track' is the Stuart Highway – with nearly as much emphasis on the word 'the' as on the word 'track'. It runs from Darwin through Katherine, Tennant Creek and Alice Springs, and then all the way down to Adelaide where you better drop the anchors or you'll end up in the ocean. When we talk about other tracks, we are talking about your regulation bush dirt roads.

So now that you are on track, let's continue down The Track – about 80 km or so – to the commencement of the Marrakai track. During the dry season, it is a fairly popular 4WD excursion that winds its way through some lovely countryside, crosses a couple of creeks and brings you out to the Arnhem Highway on the eastern side of the Adelaide River Bridge, just short of the Corroboree Park Tavern.

It had seen heavy usage a number of years before when an engineering inspection determined that the Adelaide River Bridge was in dire peril of collapsing into the croc-infested drink. For a number of months, the Marrakai track had been the main access by road, long, circuitous and unsealed as it was, from Darwin to Kakadu. There was no way we were going to get anywhere within cooee of Corroboree on today's little jolly though, those dry-season creek crossings would be expansive lakes at this time of year.

The countryside was a stunning contrast of vibrantly green, freshly washed foliage and the classic red dirt of the Top End. The sun, trying to burst through the thin layer of cloud only accentuated this luminescent effect. When images of the wet-season landscape are featured in magazine spreads, you'd be forgiven for thinking that the colour enhancement had been leaned on a bit heavily. In reality, they don't quite capture the full magnificence of the palette. It's a well-worn old chestnut, but you really do have to see it to believe it.

We made fairly decent progress along the track that was in surprisingly good nick considering the rain we had received lately. The pace was fairly leisurely; cars played a bit of hide and seek in side cuttings before reappearing behind other vehicles. Rude gestures, bared buttocks and general abuse was lobbed and volleyed back and forth between vehicles as the lead duties changed several times. We stopped occasionally at picturesque vantage points to survey the landscape, access eskies in the back trays of utes and allow smokers to indulge themselves outside the cabins of vehicles.

We had traversed a couple of very tame stretches of water across the road on the way in. I would hardly even deem to give them the title of water crossings at less than a foot in depth. When we rounded a corner and approached the Marrakai creek itself, however, that all changed. What is usually a small, meandering little feeder creek off the Adelaide River had significantly broken its banks and was now a kilometre-wide stretch of swiftly flowing, murky brown, run-off water.

We pulled off to the side and parked. As we emerged from the vehicles and took in the vast expanse of swollen creek in front of us, it was plainly obvious that this was the go-no-further point.

Tinny-boy Tim, who was along on this trip as a passenger in my vehicle, decided to do a bit of an exploratory wade. Commonly held belief states that you won't encounter crocs in rapidly flowing water. In my book, there is a very fine line between commonly held belief, urban myth and pure, undiluted bullshit. This was the Adelaide River floodplain, for God's sake. I might wade in to about ankle deep if I happened to be packing a large-calibre handgun. I was not – so did not.

Tim managed to enlist Tony, the driver of another vehicle, to join him in his display of boofhead bravado. In they went, cans in hand, calmly following the steadily shelving track down. After only 10 or so metres, they were up to the top of their thighs and the grade was continuing down. Turning around casually, they seemed oblivious to the cries of, 'Get out of there, you @#@$ idiots!'

This chorus was led by quite strident demands from Tony's very pregnant wife, Annalise, who had visions of a fatherless childhood for their firstborn. The boys maintained their nonchalant cool, however, and unhurriedly strolled back to the safety of dry land.

We all accepted there was no progress to be made past this point and so lunch was called, following which we would head back to town. As we were raiding the eskies for tucker, another two vehicles joined our convoy: an 80 series LandCruiser and a brand new, top-of-the-range SR5 HiLux.

A mother and her young child got out the passenger side of the HiLux to stretch their legs, but the driver remained at the wheel, surveying the scene. We walked up to have a chat to the bloke and advise him of our team's death-defying depth assessments. He took on board what we had to say, thought about it for two seconds, and then replied, 'I'm gonna have a crack anyway, I got a snorkel. Should be right.'

Now, Territory etiquette dictates that one bloke shouldn't tell another bloke that he's absolutely mad. A bloke has the God-given right to make stupid decisions. In fact, it is what some of us do best. Before we had the time to contemplate whether this particular situation demanded that we should possibly breach said etiquette and advise him strongly not to proceed, he was off!

He hurtled towards the swollen creek at a great rate of knots, rev count indicating that he was still in high range. Obviously favouring the get-a-run-up theory, he entered the waterway with an explosively spectacular bow wave and continued on, and down – and under.

The water level quickly crawled up the sides of the vehicle. It was well past the door seals in an instant and quickly approaching window level. Forward progress had all but ceased as the driver hurriedly raised the electric windows.

His wife and small child looked on in horrified disbelief from the vantage point they had taken up to witness Daddy's heroic adventure. She shrieked hysterically for someone to *'DO SOMETHING!'* and her panic transmitted to the baby who started wailing in sympathy.

The water licked the lip of the empty tray and the buoyancy it provided began floating the rear of the vehicle, which was then swept off its axis by the current. It was not looking good for our hero.

Without a thought (regrettably, in hindsight) Tim and Tony jumped into the tray of my HiLux. I quickly wound the hubs in, threw the boys my 10-m snap-strap from behind the back seat, and reversed into the water in low-range 4WD.

By the time we had done this, the tray of the other vehicle had filled with water and sunk. This was actually OK because it gave the vehicle some ballast. Luckily, it had also snagged itself in the upper foliage of a small, submerged roadside tree. This had momentarily delayed the swamped vehicle setting off on a submarine cruise towards the Adelaide River, with skipper still aboard.

I reversed back until my door seals were about 10 cm under and water began streaming into the cabin. The boys launched themselves into the red, murky maelstrom. Tony secured the strap to my truck while Tim attempted to hook the other loop around the tow ball of the other vehicle. The current was exerting a fair bit of drag on the broad strap and Tim was agonisingly short.

'Come back a bit more!' he yelled.

I gave him another metre and as I did, felt the back end of my vehicle start to drift. That was it for me.

Tony was closer and I shouted to him, 'All over – we're out of here!'

At that very second, Tim screamed, *'GO!'*

I engaged forward gear and only then contemplated the maths and physics of the situation. The equation went something like this. Ute with waterlogged bucket tray and probably half full inside. Approaching 3 tonnes. Likelihood of successful pull by a vehicle with severely compromised traction, itself partly submerged? Questionable.

I pushed these calculations quickly aside as the water continued streaming into the cabin and placed my faith in the trusty Tojo. The water was well over shin-deep in the front floor pan by now. I dreaded to think how much was in the back. As I let out the clutch and took up the strain, the load sat my back end down and increased my traction. Somewhat encouraged, I moved slowly forward. The tail end of the other vehicle straightened and then the whole thing began to slowly follow.

Photos taken at this point show that there was nothing of the other vehicle apart from the top section of the cabin from about halfway up the windshield protruding above the surface. Slow and steady was the go and as my vehicle continued to crawl further out of the depths, and progress became easier with each metre gained.

In fairly short order I had the shiny, new 4WD back on dry land about 30 m up the track. It was looking a little bit bedraggled and shop-soiled by now as it disgorged a deluge of dirty run-off water and a very relieved and severely embarrassed driver.

Now, I'm certainly not claiming that I was totally cool, calm and collected through the whole exercise. My clacker had been playing out a rhythmic castanet solo and my hands still shook with adrenaline.

As we all settled down and took stock of what had just actually happened, a few questions began to emerge. Primarily, why had the bloke's mate in the much more powerful Land Cruiser not come to Evel Knievel's aid?

Turns out, this bloke was Evel's brother-in-law! He said, 'I wasn't going in there. Bloke's a dickhead – always doing stuff like that.'

Charming. Glad I didn't marry into that family.

I drained my vehicle and gave everything a bit of a once-over, thanking my lucky stars he hadn't dragged me down with him – it really had been quite touch and go.

As it was, the rescued 'dickhead' never said a word to us. His wife thanked us profusely but he just drained his car, looked under the recently submerged bonnet and generally shuffled about. Tim sidled up to the bloke and said in his very understated manner, 'You do realise, fella, that my mate over there risked his truck and we risked getting washed away, to pull your stupid arse and your fifty-thousand dollar vehicle out of there? I reckon that deserves a thank you and a carton of grog at the very least, surely?'

Tim got a mumbled thank you and a fairly unconvincing promise of a carton of premium ale to be delivered to us back in town. The bloke never approached me once, the whole time.

Deciding we'd had enough adventure and arseholes for one day, we packed up our gear and headed off. As we got back onto the track to begin the homeward journey, we saw him foolishly attempt to turn the recently submerged engine over. The terminal and very expensive sound of a big end or some other major engine component being smashed through the motor block wall, followed immediately by the silence of seizure, was the inevitable result.

It was probably a total write-off now. What a pity. Brother-in-law would be forced to undertake a very long tow back to Darwin – at least he wouldn't have to put up with Evel in the cabin of the Cruiser.

I guess the motto of this tale is that sometimes, by coming to a fool's aid, you are simply circumventing the process of natural selection. Luckily, there were no major dramas with my truck, just the stink of run-off mud that permeated the cabin until the dry season. I do have a good yarn to tell and some spectacular photos of a submerged HiLux being pulled back from the brink by another, but do you reckon that bastard fronted with the slab? Course not!

Superstition

There is a spectrum associated with fishing on which all anglers can be placed. One end of this scale is marked 'skill', and at the opposite extreme, 'luck'. Those fishos situated at the skill end of the continuum rely on experience, knowledge and technique to achieve their angling goals. Loitering aimlessly at the luck end of the scale is a mob of absolutely clueless no-hopers who are totally unperturbed by their angling ignorance, but put great stock in the phrase, 'Ya never know ya luck!'

As statistical norms dictate, the great majority of fishos are to be found occupying the densely populated middle section of the bell curve situated between these two extremes. They possess varying degrees of skill, but rely heavily on luck and always hope for an oversize serving of the same.

As a general rule, those towards the skill end of the spectrum will always generate higher piscatorial returns in any scientifically controlled experiment. This reliable statistical result forms the theoretical basis of the 10 per cent of fishos catch 90 per cent of the fish rule. This does not imply, however, that the 'never know ya luck' crew will always fail to return valid data in our observational angling experiment.

Tales abound each Top End dry season of tourists fishing from a suburban boat ramp, the back deck of a haphazardly piloted houseboat, the heavily trafficked mooring pontoon of a big river or some other similarly unlikely location. The story always has them armed with a $20 chain-store rod-and-reel combo rigged with 8 lb monofilament line, a long shank whiting hook baited with a stinky chunk of twice defrosted and refrozen servo squid, and no idea of what they are doing.

At this point of the yarn, local fishos start shaking their heads, grinding their teeth and groaning inwardly because they know exactly what is coming next. I'm sure you do, too. This scenario always leads inexorably to a culmination that involves the despised interloper, in outright defiance of the laws of physics, probability and common decency, somehow managing to nail a metre-plus barramundi, the fabled metrey.

The anger, frustration and suffering of all who are forced to endure this distressing yarn is often compounded by quotes attributed to the conquering hero in the inevitable local newspaper story. 'I've only ever caught carp and toadfish before now, but this barra-fishing caper is easy! Dunno why everyone makes such a big deal of it.'

Little does our hero know that as he delightedly relishes each millisecond of his fifteen minutes of fame, there are locals plotting to lob burning tyres onto the roof of his caravan.

In my observation, there is one common trait exhibited to some degree by every inhabitant of the skill/luck angling spectrum.

Superstition. Belief in omens. Observation of bizarre rituals. Veneration of lucky talismans. A great many fishos who would, in every other aspect of their lives consider themselves to be reasoned, rational and common-sense folk, hold an unswayable belief that certain actions, inactions or incantations may visit either a blessing or a curse upon their angling prospects.

Some of these beliefs are widely held across the whole fisho population and accepted as established fact. Others are confined to a particular region or tribal grouping. Many are very personal in nature and only of relevance to the individual believer.

I am constantly amazed by this phenomenon, but that has not helped me avoid becoming entangled in the sticky tendrils of its illusory web. I don't believe in broken mirrors or black cats being harbingers of bad luck. I don't believe a bird shitting on me to be anything more than a random confluence of biological function, appropriate trajectory and coincidence of location.

However, whenever I go fishing in my boat, I pull out my lucky bone necklace (a.k.a. the boner), each segment of which is carved with a talismanic depiction of a fish. I purchased it from a Kuta Beach hawker on a Bali trip many years ago. He had a very wise and spiritual aura that belied his 12 years of age. This gave me great faith in his assurances that the necklace would bring forth a bountiful abundance of fish – and unbridled fertility as an added side bonus, all at no extra cost.

The boner receives a reverential, rosary-like rub as it is placed delicately in its designated position of maximum talismanic potency, that is, draped around my sounder. I take a moment for some quiet spiritual introspection, and then prepare myself physically and emotionally for the forthcoming bounty that has been assured by my ritual observance.

I do this openly and without any sense of shame, embarrassment or self-consciousness in front of other people. When performing this traditional ceremony, I only ever receive respectful words of encouragement from other fishos, or polite enquiries as to the significance of a particular aspect of the ritual. And even though this intensely personal act of faith and worship has no relevance for my passengers, none would dare chance putting the mockers on themselves by ridiculing someone else's particular self-delusion. Crazy!

There have been innumerable occasions where I have had my ju-ju jewellery appropriately arranged, but didn't trouble the scorer. I find other factors to blame for my lack of success on these occasions. When I do happen to get among some fish, however, I rub my talisman fondly and mumble heartfelt words of thanksgiving.

If I were to perform just such a ritual outside the newsagent before purchasing my lotto tickets or before the kick-off of a TV football game I desperately wanted my team to win, my mates would call me mad as a cut snake. I would be relentlessly ridiculed and possibly totally alienated lest this strange hippy madness infect them. It really is crazy!

I know of another bloke who keeps a dog-eared adult publication preserved for posterity in a clip-seal bag stored delicately under his casting deck. He was perusing this particular piece of photo literature when he latched onto a massive 60-cm mangrove jack live-baiting in a harbour arm a number of years before. The pages are water damaged and stuck together in places (from bait residue of course, what were *you* thinking?) but he believes his chances are greatly enhanced by having it safe and sound, even if unseen, stashed in the nose of his boat.

I know another skipper who demands that the first quarter of the first can of the trip from every crew member be drained onto the floor of the boat as an offering to the fish gods.

I myself maintain a strict policy of always throwing back the first 'keeper' barra of an extended trip. I do this to honour the inhabitants of the waterway on which I will be flicking, and curry favour with the fishing gods that they may see their way clear to grant me my wish of a hundred-fold return on such a gesture of goodwill.

Probably the most widely held and stringently enforced fishin' superstition centres on the banana. For centuries, bananas have been held responsible for poor catches and maritime mishaps. There are a number of theories as to where this old chestnut originated. Some say that boats in the Caribbean transporting bananas had to sail as quickly as possible to avoid their cargo going off. This made their trolling quite ineffective, and hence, no fish.

Another theory is that bunches of bananas were invariably riddled with venomous spiders and once a ship had transported a load, it too was infested. From this point it was only a matter of time before the crew would fall foul of their evil webs of doom and succumb to a horrible and agonising death.

My favourite theory, though, runs purely along the old slapstick line. Bananas on a boat meant banana skins on the deck – which meant people slipping comically overboard to a watery demise.

The curse of the 'nana is still taken very seriously to this day. Charter-boat crews will check the bags of paying customers before leaving dock for this most forbidden of fruit. A veto often extends to such processed presentations as banana cake, and even the miniature, yellow, lolly versions that have no actual banana content whatsoever. Even this confectionery effigy of the loathed fruit is apparently enough to invoke the horrific consequences of the curse.

I myself flagrantly disregard the banana ban. My firmly held belief that bananas pose absolutely no impediment to successful fishing whatsoever stems back to an episode on Yellow Water quite a few years ago. I was enjoying a leisurely troll along a lily line when I nearly choked on the banana I had been enjoying. I literally inhaled the fruit whole when an 86-cm barra did the same thing to my lure. I managed to swallow most of the banana, spray the rest of it around the inside of my boat and over my passenger, and then successfully land the fish. Proof positive!

The astounding array of superstitions displayed by fishermen across the land ironically highlights the glaring ridiculousness of the whole superstition concept. It's quite OK for you to pick and choose which superstitions you believe in, which rituals you observe, and which events constitute a good, or conversely bad, omen. You can then reject out of hand those that don't suit you. Should the predominant superstitions on offer not quite fill your requirements, or if you prefer a more rigorously ju-ju-ed and mojo-ed existence, there is plenty of scope to simply make up your own superstition from scratch.

Psychologists believe that a rigid adherence to a superstition can have a placebo-like effect. If we carry our lucky talisman or perform our lucky ritual, it fuels an attitude of positive thought and this is what can be instrumental in achieving success. I say, crap! I have run the whole gamut of mental attitudes as psychological preparation regimes and they are uniformly unsuccessful – with one notable exception. Let me run you through them.

Overtly positive – this involves loudly and exuberantly predicting a resounding success in the imminent angling venture. Confidently and repeatedly proclaiming to all within earshot that a bounty in size, number and species is about to be mercilessly harvested. In adopting this approach, one must maintain a slavish commitment to a total and unshakeable belief in the power of the self-fulfilling prophecy. There is an inherent tendency to burn bridges in the overtly positive approach, deliberately leaving one's self no escape route should the venture fail: 'Right. I've been such a massive pain in the arse so full of cocky confidence that the consequences of failure will be unthinkably horrific. Now I have no other option but to live up to my claims.'

A successful overtly positive campaign demands the most fervent self-belief and positive mental attitude. You bet heavily, the whole bankroll in fact, that if you really, *really* believe it – it really will happen. Unfortunately though, life is not a Mary Poppins screenplay. The overtly positive approach is by far the most psychologically scarring when the predicted bounty fails to materialise. Not only do you have the crushing disappointment of your own unfulfilled expectations, but there is also the scornful ridicule heaped upon you from those exacting revenge for the tirade of tiresomely over-inflated optimism you lambasted them with prior to the fact.

Tacitly positive – bearing many of the traits of overtly positive, but largely internalised, tacitly positive operates on a very intimate, personal level. Fishos often adopt this method of mental preparation after suffering the psychological trauma resulting from an overtly positive episode that has ended badly.

Tacitly positive works towards integrating all aspects of your conscious self to become unerringly aligned with your specific angling goal. There are no manic displays of confidence as evident in the overt. The only outward manifestation of a successful tacit preparation may be an enigmatic smile and a faraway look in the eye, or possibly a very understated, 'Yeah, I reckon we might do alright.'

Internally though, hope reigns supreme. There is a belief in the tacit that any verbalisation of their expectant optimism may possibly break the spell and dash their chances. Their belief is an article of faith, an intimate, solemn contract between themselves and the higher spiritual beings that determine all angling outcomes.

When the tacit preparation does lead to a positive outcome, the fisho experiences a euphoric sense of enlightened fulfilment and self-congratulation. They may be tempted to go a little overt in response, but this tendency must be kept firmly in check. An unseemly celebration may potentially cruel future successful tacit outcomes.

On the other hand, a failure following a well-implemented tacit preparation is often a soul-rending experience and emotionally debilitating. The sense of betrayal can be absolute. 'Why, after my unerring faith and silent devotion have you chosen to spurn me? Why, Why, WHY!' The inner turmoil and emotional angst generated by this catastrophe of conviction often leads one to the next natural step in this karmic progression.

Abject pessimism – 'Here we go again. Baked by sun, pounded by rain, monstered by biting insects and, for what? Nothing! I dunno why I bother.'

There are a number of convoluted rationales that lead one to adopt this very negative approach. One line of thought borrows from the theory of reverse psychology. Because neither of the positive mental attitudes produced the desired result, the extreme opposite may well be thc answer.

There is also the vain hope that the fishing gods may take pity on such a wretched soul and grant them an unexpected bonus. Alternatively, there is the perception that these same gods work strictly along Bastards Incorporated guidelines and make the exact opposite of what you expect come to pass.

Some operate on this abject pessimism principle purely as a self-preservation mechanism. So cruelly scarred are they by the devastating disappointment of previous failures that they are not even game to hope for good things lest that fledgling hope be once again resoundingly crushed. There is a deluded belief that if you start out with expectations of failure and fiasco, you will not be surprised or despondent when these results eventuate. This is a dangerously destructive misconception.

A particularly poor result while operating in abject pessimism mode can drive one down into a very dark psychological place indeed, well below what you thought was the baseline of disappointment. These fishos find themselves in a melancholic mire of bitter recrimination, self-loathing and gnashing of teeth. I can tell you this from experience, readers. I have wallowed in this vile emotional hell numerous times.

This is the nadir that breaks many fishos and sends them scurrying to place classified ads and visit pawnbrokers. They divest themselves completely of their hard-collected and previously cherished angling arsenal in a moment of maudlin madness.

Some shattered souls even resort to a backyard bonfire, symbolically incinerating their angling accoutrement. (The furnace a metaphor for the living hell in which they find themselves interred.) Boat, rods, tackle, everything must go! It is a drastic and tragic response to a drastic and tragic circumstance. The emotionally damaged fisho will do anything at this point to make the pain go away.

There is a fourth state of mind that in my opinion, is the only one that actually produces tangible results. Quite predictably, it is an immensely difficult mindset to achieve. Many claim that it is in fact impossible for the human psyche to truly and effectively maintain.

* * *

Disinterested nonchalance – on a superficial level, it is very easy to appear disinterestedly nonchalant. You may say things like, 'Ah, y' know. I don't really care, actually. Just heading out for a bit of a look around,' but internally, you are harbouring varying degrees of either positive or negative outlook. It is psychologically unavoidable. While you are in any way consciously addressing your angling prospects, there is a vestige of leaning one way or another, and possibly a blend of both.

It is only when your mind drifts to other totally unrelated matters (such as your football team's poor current form, mentally undressing the new checkout attendant at your local corner shop, or putting the finishing touches on your fiendish plot to kill your work supervisor in what could only be described as the perfect murder), that true nonchalance is actually achieved and results begin to flow.

How many times have you sat for hours primed like a cobra ready to strike at the slightest indication of interest in your line? Your steely gaze so intent and unwavering that you find it hard to believe that fish are not stunned to the surface by your sheer force of will. All to no avail, but put the rod down to scratch your nether regions, get a beer or something to eat out of the esky, or perhaps even indulge in a little nap instead – and all hell breaks loose! The fish chooses this very moment to launch an aggressive surprise assault, because you have momentarily, unconsciously developed a natural state of disinterested nonchalance!

I like to use an analogy that is strictly from a bloke's perspective, but probably works just as effectively with the roles reversed. Fish are like women. They have finely tuned sensors that can accurately detect desperation, eagerness and yearning desire from a great distance. They find the aroma abhorrent. When angling to hook up with a female of the human species, there is no better way to elicit a response of total disinterest, or even active scorn, than to prance around with puppy-like enthusiasm – tongue out, eager to please, prepared to do anything for a pat. You stink of desperation and she despises you for it.

Conversely, if you stand at the bar adopting an attitude of studied indifference – bored, aloof and unavailable – you quickly make yourself an object of interest. Your disinterested nonchalance is irresistible to your prey and there is every chance you will get a wholeheartedly aggressive strike.

This chapter has, in essence, been an unsuccessful attempt to quantify the great angling intangibles. It has probably left you with more questions than answers, more fable than fact, more excrement than explanation.

Skill, luck, mojo, ju-ju, positive mental attitude – I don't know. What I *do* know is that fishing is a mind game that has the potential to become a minefield primed to detonate in your psyche given one false step.

The run-off

THE. RUN. OFF. Three simple, single syllable words that taken in isolation, have no great significance, impact or power in and of themselves. When these three individually innocuous words are combined in the right sequence, however, they suddenly acquire an intangible yet unbridled power to bewitch, enchant and possess the Top End angler.

This 'possession' may not actually reach the stage where a fisho's head spins around on his shoulders while spewing forth streams of demonically inspired green bile. It does undeniably set their minds spinning though – and they do spew forth rivers of undiluted 'brown'.

For barra fishermen, the run-off is an all-consuming preoccupation. It provokes endless theoretical proposition, insightful analysis and tactical discussion. Gut feeling, blind optimism and wishful thinking also make a significant contribution.

Smoko small talk, BBQ banter, exchanges by the workplace water cooler and conversations resulting from chance encounters in the street – all are dominated by this mythical, magical, maniacal phase of the annual fishing cycle: when will it start; what set of tides or conditions will be the trigger; what are the prospects; which catchment holds the most water; which river will be first to fire?

The run-off's influence is not just confined to the barra-fishing fraternity. Significant social, economic and industrial implications are felt by the wider Top End community. Productivity plummets as tradesmen, service technicians, sales reps, bank managers, medical and therapeutic professionals, financial advisers, lawn-mowing contractors and even politicians are all mysteriously uncontactable: phones 'switched off, or not in a mobile service area'.

Office workers spend a large portion of their days planning the logistics of their run-off sorties. They stare wistfully into space as they visualise the gore and glory of the coming adventure, or alternatively doze through the day as they recuperate from their extra-curricular exertions.

There is a pronounced spike in the presentation of mysterious 'lurgies' with widely varied but non-specific symptoms, generally blamed on change-of-season conditions. When sick-leave data is analysed in association with a lunar chart for the period, this apparent epidemic seems to ebb and flow in synchronisation with tidal and moon phases – most curious!

Family relationships come under heavy strain as lonely, confused and distressed children ask of frustrated, seasonally sole parents, 'Why is Daddy (or Mummy) never home? Doesn't he (or she) like us anymore?' The abandoned spouse struggles for an answer – and often silently asks herself (or himself) the same question.

The run-off. Obviously a force of nature to contend with, but what exactly is it? To draw a bit of a mud map for you, we need to reference both the seasonal calendar of the tropical north, and the sexual calendar of *Lates calcarifer,* a.k.a. the barramundi.

During the monsoonal phase of the Top End's wet, the floodplains around the big rivers and smaller coastal estuaries of the Northern Territory are awash with seasonal floodwaters. The soil, that was only recently parched and cracked from the dry-season bake, has now reached saturation level and will absorb no more.

The staggering monsoonal deluge pummels down from on high and results in thousands of square kilometres of submerged floodplain. These tepid, nutrient-rich waters provide a magnificently expansive nursery for all sorts of species, both micro and macro, to spawn and multiply.

The barramundi have spent the wet season hard at it. On the job. Doing the jiggy-jig. The exertions of the spawning season have left them lean, mean – and hungry. Now that their small minds have been cleared of procreative priorities, they prepare to focus on satisfying the demands of their other driving appetite, and go seriously on the chew.

The fisho, on the other hand, has his angling activities largely curtailed during the monsoonal period, so spends his time earning good behaviour tokens to be cashed in during the coming run-off. Postponed maintenance chores are seen to. Dodgy split rings and trebles on lures are replaced, reels are serviced, cracked rod runners also replaced then rebound. The newly reconditioned lures are fastidiously categorised and stored according to colour, depth, length and favoured status criteria.

When all these tasks are completed, fishos begin pacing, climbing the walls and driving their other half to distraction with their twitching anticipation of the imminent fishy fireworks.

Then, as the monsoon recedes, the delicious, seething protein soup of bugs, frogs, tadpoles, baitfish, crustaceans and a whole host of other barra goodies that have been brewing on the floodplains for months, begin to empty back into the rivers proper. This is it. The run-off!

Barramundi and barra fishos alike go absolutely womba. The frenetic onslaught of the barramundi's post-coital feeding frenzy is matched and often surpassed by the exuberance of the fisho's. Liberated from their cabin fever by the receding waters, they are possessed with a blood lust that demands to be sated. A single-minded, tunnel-visioned preoccupation overcomes both predator and prey.

A feverish rumour mill comes into play and holds Darwin and other Top End towns in its whispering grip. Everybody is listening in on everyone else: muttered boasts, eavesdropped insights, reliable, red-hot tips and unsubstantiated, outright bullshit all circulate virally. Reports that may initially have been accurate and without embellishment get so heavily distorted with each retelling that by the time they get to third or fourth hand, they bear no resemblance to the original tale whatsoever. Fishos are quite aware of this, but will listen with interest and pass the Chinese whisper on to their network nonetheless – adding their own slight distortion in the passage, of course. It's a fever, a fixation, an all-consuming obsession.

Fisher folk will do whatever it takes to be able to join in the run-off fray. Formerly diligent and reliable workers ring in sick with flimsy, fanciful explanations. Honest folk will lie, steal and cheat. Otherwise devoted spouses will spurn, deceive and desert their partners. Professional pillars of society will wantonly desert their posts and essential duties without giving so much as a fig for the consequences.

The run-off generally takes place between March and May, depending on the magnitude of the preceding wet. The mouth of the Mary River system is often the first to fire and a primary point of focus. Small coastal creeks such as Love, Carmour, Swim and Marsh are targeted on the big spring tides. The preferred neap-tide methodology involves trolling the massive tannin outflows into Chambers Bay supplied by the more substantial Tommycut and Sampan creeks. The large number of boats trolling here during the peak of the run-off earns it the name, 'the conga line'.

The Daly River probably rivals the Mary system in run-off pre-eminence, producing vast numbers of big silver fish as the flood level drops. It is a big, long river, which is just as well because there can be hundreds of boats spread out along its winding path, flicking the many feeder creeks spewing colour back into the main channel.

Colour change is what fishos are looking for in these rivers. The tea-coloured water of floodplain run-off contrasts sharply with the iced-coffee colour of the main body of water. Barra lie in wait in the iced coffee, ready to ambush bait washed out in the tea. Flicking lures along the colour change will inevitably see you get smashed!

The mouths of the other major rivers – the East and South Alligators, the Roper and the Adelaide – also begin to go off. The method on these rivers is much the same: look for bait and colour in feeder creeks. Often these rivers will fire closer to the mouths earlier in the run-off, then the focus shifts further upstream as the water levels drop and the river re-enters its dry-season banks.

Though obviously at its peak during the actual time of the run-off, this magic and manic season's power to transfix reaches far beyond the point where the rivers return to normal. The run-off that has just been will be discussed at great length for months to come. Retrospective reviews, detailed deconstructions and analytical assessments will take place. While the recent run-off is fresh in one's mind this is the perfect time to begin planning next year's assault armed with the wisdom of hindsight.

Sometimes the run-off can be cruelly curtailed to only one or two tidal cycles, other years it will continue for months. But before you know it – and certainly before you've caught what you consider to be your fair quota of barra – the run-off from the floodplains slows to a trickle and then ceases altogether.

On your way home from the last sortie of your run-off campaign, you might even notice some thin, wispy clouds in the sky, or possibly pass a car and caravan combo, or Britz behemoth.

Suddenly, it is the dry.

Commando bling

Jeremy Harmsworth and Paul Van Bruggen – or Harmsy and PVB as they are known to The Tinny – are two pretty-hardcore Darwin fishos. Both are very accomplished practitioners of the angling arts, but this tale from out of The Tinny goes to prove that even the most experienced can come horribly unstuck.

PVB is a noted bowerbird, a collector of angling accoutrement. He likes trinkets, he can afford trinkets and there is always a new trinket to buy. He currently runs about 30 separate rods with matched reels and an arsenal of lures, jigs and associated tackle. When he says, 'In my tackle box …' he is actually referring to his purpose-built, over-dimension shed. In this 'tackle box', he houses his large boat, his large collection of rods and his large collection of lures – hung row upon row in blocks of similar depth, size and target species.

Now Paul won't mind me saying he was pretty much 'over dimension' himself at the time this yarn is set. He has lost a shed-load (or should that be a tackle box?) of kilos since and is now a strapping, whippet-like figure, well, sort of, but at the time, he too was quite … large.

Paul and Harmsy were out on the harbour in PVB's boat doing a bit of bottom bouncing. (When fishing the bottom for reef dwelling fish in the Top End, a large sinker or 'snapper lead' is required to hold position against the strong tidal current. As the boat rises and falls on gentle swells, the lead lifts off and drops back to the sea floor, which can be felt through the line – hence 'bottom bouncing'.) They weren't too far from shore, anchored up on one of the rocky outcrops that ring Darwin's CBD and fishing for pan-sized snapper. They were not all that serious, really, just having a bit of a fish and giggle and enjoying the opportunity to be on the water.

With lines in the water, but rods racked conveniently in holders, they discussed matters of great importance and resolved weighty issues confronting modern Australia, as was their wont. Paul was test-running a brand new piece of 'bling' he had recently acquired. Bling was PVB's slang for a suitably sparkly and attractive rod or reel. He had further customised this particular rig for its maiden outing with the addition of a shiny gold power knob. This process was known as bling enhancement.

The boys had been kicking around several quite weighty social issues, and dealing with the thirst that was a direct result of these negotiations, when the conversation was brought to an abrupt halt. PVB's rod arced over quite violently and started to peel line.

As menioned Paul was at the time a big fella but still very agile – before he could get to the rod though, disaster struck. The rod holder cracked and gave way under the strain. The brand-new, shiny piece of bling whipped over the side and began a fish-assisted descent into Darwin Harbour.

In a lightning-fast reflexive action, PVB dived overboard and made a lunging, desperate grasp for the shimmering gold power knob that was rapidly receding from sight into the briny. In the instant that he was airborne – between the leap and hitting the water – he noticed Harmsy in a similar mid-air dive pose. Though thinking, 'Oops, this is not good,' he couldn't help the mental image forming of just how this frozen moment in time would appear to others – like a flying, tumbling mid-air confrontation from a Hong Kong kung-fu film between a samurai and a sumo wrestler.

Paul speared into the water with arms outstretched. His fingers came into contact with the magnificent gilt handle which he grasped with grim determination. Broaching the surface with a desperately gasping inhalation of air, he held his prize triumphantly aloft like the lady of the lake preparing to bestow the mighty Excalibur on Arthur. As he saw his partner in crime resurface beside him, all sense of triumph and amusement evaporated as the reality of the situation sank in: both he and Harmsy were in the water, there was a big tide running and the boat was already rapidly diminishing in size as they were swept seaward.

'I didn't plan on going in, it was a total reflex. I saw the rod go in and I just followed,' said Paul.

Harmsy recounted, 'Never in a million years did I think Paul would go in – but there we were, both of us in the drink making good progress towards Timor.'

By the time PVB had surfaced, the boat was already 5 m away. 'I made a frantic effort to swim back to the boat but the current ripped my daks off and they got tangled around my legs so I couldn't kick.'

PVB continued, 'Then I realised that the fish that had caused this strife in the first place was still on the end of the bloody rod! It was dragging me even further away.'

PVB handed the rod over to Harmsy as he floated past. PVB's larger frame on which the tide could gain purchase, combined with his inability to kick effectively, resulted in him floating off at a greater rate of knots than Harmsy.

Luckily, a hire boat full of young blokes had not been far away and they had seen the whole potentially life-threatening, but undeniably comical episode unfold. They roared over to make good the rescue.

Paul tells how they approached him first. 'I warned 'em I had no daks on. I thought it was only fair that they should prepare themselves mentally for the horror of what was about to unfold,' Paul chuckled. 'They pulled me up onto the transom and I managed to get myself back into a state of respectable dress, much to the relief of everyone on board. Then we turned to pick up Harmsy.'

'I shouted to them that I still had the fish on,' Harmsy continued. 'I'm sure they thought I was mad, but when I started getting dragged off again, they realised I was fair dinkum and chucked a life buoy at me. Pretty funny really, only ever seen them used in cartoons!' Harmsy clung to the bright-orange ring, got dragged back to the boat and handed the rod up.

When asked whether he wanted to land the fish himself, PVB replied, 'The bastard just about drowned me, so I better try and finish this battle on top!'

He continued fighting the fish as Harmsy clambered aboard the hire boat. Eventually, a 6-kg cod showed itself to be the cause of all the kerfuffle and was successfully boated. The rescue crew were in a state of stunned disbelief.

'They couldn't believe our commitment!' Harmsy chuckled as the boys recounted the tale later over a cold ale.

PVB adds, 'Dunno about commitment – most people I tell reckon we should be committed!'

Probably right, Paul. Once again, I refer you to Rule number one.

Crocs! (Geoff)

GEOFF BOLITHO IS a bloke from Jabiru who works at the Ranger Uranium mine and fishes a lot. In fact, that's a pretty accurate one-line descriptor for a fair proportion of the Jabiru population – except for the Geoff Bolitho part, of course, there's only one of him.

Jabiru is a town that was initially established by the mining giant ERA, and is still owned and run by them to service the Ranger Uranium mine just outside of town. It's right in the heart of Kakadu National Park. Not everyone works directly for Ranger, but it is pretty much the sole reason the town exists.

If you happen to be tied up in the mining game and are also partial to a bit of fishin', there could hardly be a better posting on the planet than Jabiru. You have easy access to great billabong-style fishing at spots such as Red Lily, Bucket and Alligator billabongs as well as the famously picturesque, but still highly productive, Yellow Waters.

The mighty South and East Alligator rivers are right on your doorstep. Both are magnificent barramundi-producing estuaries that in turn provide access to fantastic coastal and blue-water fisheries. The pristine wilderness of Arnhem Land is but a spear's throw away, and even roadside drains and culverts become productive fisheries during the peak of the wet season. The town has a great bakery so there's loaves to go with your fishes and they do a good pie. What more could you possibly want?

Having done my bit for the Jabiru Town Council and the Kakadu Tourism Board, let's return to Geoff, who has the distinction, or misfortune, of being at the centre of this particular yarn.

Geoff and a couple of mates, Paul Eddy and his dad, Jeff, were on an extended trip on the East Alligator River. To avoid confusion here, we'll call Paul's dad Jeff Snr, even though he is a J.E.F.F.

The boys intended to mix up a bit of bottom bouncing out the front with some barra fishing in the river itself. They had been working blue-water reefs and bommies (rocky outcrops on the sea bed) between the East Alligator mouth and Murgenella for a couple of days, chasing predominantly golden snapper.

The fishing out there had proved to be pretty productive and they were eating their fill of prime, fresh goldy fillets each night. They were keen to get out of the wind and wash the salty crust off themselves though, so decided the time was right to poke up river. Getting onto a few big barra would put the icing on the cake of an already pretty good trip, they reckoned.

The plan was to head up to Magella Creek that feeds into the East about 60 km or so upstream from the mouth. When the upper reaches of Magella Creek floods, it blocks road access to Cahill's Crossing and the East Alligator boat ramps for a large proportion of the wet season. The road often remains under two or more metres of water for considerable periods, so many fishos will take the long way around. This entails driving to the South Alligator River and launching there, going 80 or so kilometres downstream to the mouth, then 30 km across open water to the mouth of the East, and then upstream to have a crack at Magella.

The fact that people are willing to spend this much time and effort and burn the substantial amount of fossil fuel required for the task is an indicator of just how highly regarded Magella Creek is as a premier run-off hotspot. Large amounts of tannin water rich with juicy, tasty barra lollies, sluices into the river off the floodplains during run-off times. Barra know it and fishos know that barra know it. Cricket scores of run-off barra boated and released are not uncommon both inside this famous creek and at its junction with the East Alligator proper.

The boys motored upriver to Magella and turned into the creek to push towards the upper reaches approaching the floodplains. After a quick fish at a few feeder creeks that only produced a couple of 'rats' (undersize barra), dark was approaching so they anchored up at a likely looking junction for the evening. Knackered from their travels and the previous couple of days' exposure to saltwater bluster, they were looking forward to a good feed and a solid kip in preparation for a fair dinkum crack at the barra the next day.

They were in Paul's 5.3 m plate boat that was quite comfortable for the three of them. After anchoring, they took turns to perch on the duckboard and avail themselves of a much-anticipated fresh-water rinse with the deck wash and carry out other general ablutions. The process resulted in all three declaring themselves to be 'a new man'!

As dark set in, they went into lock-down mode to avoid the imminent assault by flying, biting vermin. This involved hoisting the bimini top and lowering the custom-made insect screens that fixed securely to the gunwales of the boat. This masterstroke of innovative design made for a magnificently secure and comfortable environment to spend the night in an otherwise potentially life-threatening insect environment.

The biting heat of the day had receded somewhat, the boys felt refreshed and revitalised after a wash, and the beers started to slide down quite nicely. After a quiet couple, kitchen duties were assigned and the evening meal cooked, consumed and commented on favourably. The trio relaxed and settled in for a yarn and a couple more ales in the soft glow of the anchor light. Jeff Snr was sitting in the skipper's chair, Paul was on his bum on the casting deck up forward and Geoff was beside him on a folding deckchair.

The hull of Paul's boat flares up considerably towards the nose so the gunwales are very high and about 200 mm wide. They double as very functional drink or elbow rests, and Paul was using one of them for both these purposes.

It had been a pretty big couple of days and it was decided one more would wrap up proceedings nicely before hitting the swags in preparation for the next day's much-anticipated barra assault. They were about halfway through the last can, and mid-point in earnest conversation when out of the blue, or more accurately, out of the black, all hell broke loose.

An almighty *SPLASH! THUD! BANG!* and Geoff was smacked in the shoulder with considerable force. Bowled over onto the lower deck of the tinny, he landed sprawled out at Paul's feet. It was all over in an instant. A stunned silence returned, momentarily.

Geoff shook his head and tried to take stock of what had just taken place. Jeff Snr said he had seen a vague flash of something white sliding back over the gunwale after all the hullabaloo. As Geoff got back to his feet, he realised he had a sore head and blood coming down his arm. 'Shit! It had to be a croc!' was the consensus of opinion.

The reflection of the anchor light off the inside of the insect mesh stopped them from seeing anything outside the boat, so they arced up the big spotty for a bit of a scout around and carefully raised the mesh, extremely wary of a possible secondary assault.

Sure enough, just on the other side of the junction was a croc at around the 4-m mark. It glared at them defiantly and made no effort whatsoever to sink from sight or move on. Discretion is undeniably the better part of valour in dealing with crocodiles, and our heroes decided the best way to win this particular argument was to simply run away – as fast as possible.

Luckily, they hadn't rolled out the swags or moved stuff around in preparation for the night's kip, so it was just a matter of pulling anchor. As they performed the three-point turn required to get back out to the main body of the East, the croc just stood its ground and continued to hold them in its malevolent stare.

The boys are all long-time Territorians and frequent fishers, so they encounter crocs all the time. The behaviour of this cranky bugger was not usual. A creepy chill went up their spines as they idled as quietly and unobtrusively as possible past their attacker and off downstream, happy to concede the junction to its overly aggressive occupant.

They motored all the way back to the ramp in the dark, arriving about midnight. It was only then, upon regaining the relative safety of dry land, that they really took stock of events. Geoff had a couple of holes torn in the arm and shoulder section of his shirt and some matching scratches, bruises and abrasions on his shoulder and upper arm. There was also one single puncture mark right in the middle of the top of his head. A bit of claret had flowed, but all the wounds were relatively superficial. The mozzie dome was also a bit the worse for wear, but the combination of the mesh and the support strap for the bimini had probably saved Geoff's life by throwing the projectile croc off target just a bit.

After strapping the boat on the trailer they headed back into Jabiru, arriving home about 1 am. Next morning, Geoff reported the incident to the local park rangers who first reckoned it must have been a toey little fella that had launched itself at them. The boys politely disagreed. Once the rangers came and had a look at Geoff and the boat, and they started recreating events in the cold light of day, the numbers and distances didn't stack up for the culprit to be an acrobatic, angry little bugger.

The distance between the puncture marks on Geoff's shoulder and the top of his head indicated a considerable span of jaw opening. Paul's boat is of a make that is renowned for their large amount of freeboard. This height above the waterline is even greater towards the bow where Geoff was seated because of the gunwale's upward flare. Measuring from the waterline to where he had been sitting in a forensic re-enactment-type scenario, they conservatively calculated the croc must have had between 1.6 m and 1.9 m of its body out of the water at the moment of its mistimed crack at Geoff. If it were only a 2-m or even a 3-m croc, it would've ended up in the boat with them.

Now genuinely concerned about the situation, the rangers made preparations for a night mission down to Magella themselves. Night-time is the best time to chase crocs because of their giveaway reflective eyes. They motored up Magella that night and right in the exact junction described by the boys, they found a large croc behaving very strangely and aggressively. It approached their boat in a determined, attack-like way that sealed its fate.

The rangers couldn't take a chance with this fella. He was obviously having significant anger-management and trespass-intolerance issues. It would only be a matter of time, and by all indications a short matter of time, before it had a go at another fisho, or possibly even the rangers themselves as they went about their business on the river.

They threw an extremely high-velocity, lead projectile at the croc that brought the game to a sudden end. They then harpooned it and dragged it aboard. When they laid it out it went just under the 4-m mark and probably weighed well over 500 kg.

So Geoff lives to tell the tale. An absolute cracking tale it is too of 'How I got bit on the head by a 4-m croc and lived to tell the tale!' Does he still fish? Of course he does. It would take more than a glancing flesh wound from a monster lizard to scare a hardened Territorian fisho off the job. He did, however, significantly upgrade the size of his own boat and now keeps his deckchair slap bang in the middle of the deck.

Religion

Religion is a broad church. Isn't it, fishos? There's such a wide choice of good stuff to believe in! You've got all your common franchises like Christianity, Judaism, Islam, Buddhism, Amway and Tupperware, all trying to spread their particular gospel, convert heathens and open new branches in unpreached territory.

Then there are those who occupy the slightly unorthodox periphery, peddling (or in some cases, pedalling) their spiritual wares from the bike path just off to the side of the mainstream highway to heaven – Jehova's Witnesses, Mormons, Hare Krishnas, Scientologists and the like.

I even know of a bloke who worships a power pole on the Arnhem Highway about 25 km past the Humpty Doo Tavern. He believes his deity delivers divine prophecies, spiritual enlightenment, moral guidance and the winning Saturday night lotto numbers in the form of epiphanous oscillations of the high-voltage wires. I will concede that this bloke has had a considerable amount of divine chemical intervention in his time, but who am I to say he's wrong?

Many of the 'mainstream' religions such as Christianity consider the 'alternatives', Scientology for example, to be whacko fringe dwellers with doctrine based on fantasy and fiction. But when you look at it, there is a fair bit of 'pot calling the kettle black' involved here – or possibly even 'heathen crying heresy'?

One of these mainstream religions believes in a bloke who was conceived of a virgin birth. He healed lepers, cripples and the blind willy-nilly. He walked on water, and also turned water to wine, and a handful of breadcrumbs and fish scraps into 5 000 salmon sangers. Finally, in what must be regarded as the all-time, ultimate party trick, he resurrected himself after lying dead under a rock for three days, and then bailed up his mates at his own wake. What an absolute cracker!

To this day he still appears to his flock in birthmarks, deformed pieces of fruit and burnt toast. He has the power to makes statues of himself bleed from the hands, feet and flank, and effigies of his dear old mum weep miraculous tears of sorrow.

The other mob believe that seventy-five million years ago there was a bloke called Xenu who was the dictator of a galactic confederacy. Things were going a bit awry for Xenu, so he enlisted the help of evil psychiatrists to drug and freeze billions of his people. He flew them to Earth in DC–8s, stacked them around volcanoes and killed them by detonating big mobs of hydrogen bombs. The spirits of these nuked aliens tried to float off into the atmosphere, but Xenu wasn't going to have any of that and built an electric fence to keep them trapped on Earth. These poor souls were understandably pissed off at this succession of unpleasant events and as a result, their aggro essences hang around to this very day causing us spiritual harm.

The only way to cleanse yourself and progress through the operating levels of this particular stairway to heaven is to donate all your cash to the church. The church hierarchy puts about rumours (but strangely, not guarantees) that when you get to the top operating levels you attain super powers. You need to be able to throw barrow-loads of loot at the church to get anywhere near this level though, so it helps if you are a movie star or something like that. Dunno, but I reckon my old mate who listens to the high-voltage power poles for lotto numbers is looking positively rational at this juncture ...

Religion is basically a set of cultural belief systems that gives meaning to life and guides the adherent's philosophy, morality, lifestyle and ethics. Many religions have strong symbolism associated with traditional practices and rituals. Clerical hierarchies and worshippers often distinguish themselves by wearing bizarre and fanciful attire and headwear. Veneration of colourful talismans and trinkets is common and ceremonial staffs (or rods), often have a place in the worship ritual.

Is the picture becoming clearer, fishos? Can you see the ecstatic image starting to take form on the spiritual sounder? Behold, as the divine anchor light of revelation beats back the darkness of despair and godlessness to guide you towards an epiphanous understanding!

Yea, verily I say unto thee: *piscis reprehendo est monastica.* Fishing *is* religion! I deliver to you from on high, like tablets from

Mt Sinai, Anglercism! The Church of Fishianity! Praise be to Rod! May the Lord Al-mullety have mercy on fishing holes. Let he who is without bait cast the first net. Blessed be the fisho father, son and whole esky of beer and spirits.

Fishing provides a philosophical, ethical and spiritual guide to our lives. It determines our lifestyle, behaviour and demeanour. It gives meaning to an otherwise pointless, directionless and pagan existence.

We devoutly attend 'services' most weekends, worshipping at far-flung and disparate churches across the land – estuarine abbeys, saltwater synagogues, mangrove mosques and on the vast basilica of blue water. We make sacrificial offerings of tackle, time and legal tender to demonstrate our undying devotion.

Our faith sustains us through the adverse conditions and lean times that are sent to try us, secure in the knowledge that we are doing the good and righteous work of the almighty. We maintain a faith that glorious reward will be ours at a time and tide of our fishy lord's mysterious choosing.

We congregate with others who share the same beliefs to swap tales of salvation, enlightenment and divine intervention. We gargle consecrated altar wine, rejoice in our shared faith and sometimes, after a little too much rejoicing and gargling, we speak in tongues and have out-of-body experiences. Praise be to Rod!

Like all churches, the congregation of Anglercism is made up of a very 'catholic' collection of folk. There are those who were born into the faith and have observed a life-long adherence to the practices and rituals that form the guiding tenets of their spiritual existence. They generally go about their worship in a quiet and unassuming manner, comfortable with their belief and devotion, and at one with their articles of faith.

Then there are the part-time parishioners. While truly believing in the divine teachings and spiritual values of the Church of Fishianity, these folk only find time to actually worship on holidays or the odd long-weekend a couple of times a year. On these occasions, they often try and indoctrinate their children into the faith as some form of atonement for their own lack of piety.

Reconnecting with their own almost-forgotten faith, and seeing the beatific rapture of religious revelation in the eyes of their children, they are filled with a sense of holy communion and spiritual rebirth. They promise themselves they will be more devout in future and build on this cornerstone of re-established connection with the transcendent.

The busy grind of everyday modern life soon intervenes, however, and the conviction and commitment slowly fades from memory to become nothing more than an infrequent, guilty niggle at the conscience between Sunday morning golf games.

There is also a curious segment of the Angler-can congregation that has no religious conviction at all. They often attend worship, and may even take part in the rituals, but there is no emotional, spiritual or devotional connection whatsoever. These atheistic folk do not *believe*, but are forced to maintain a facade of faith due to a complication in their domestic situation: these lost souls have had the misfortune of becoming romantically entangled with a devotee of Fishianity when they themselves are non-believers.

This is a cruel, emotionally conflicting position in which to find one's self – loving the person but despising the belief. Many of these angling agnostics delude themselves that if they bide their time until the emotional commitment is firmly cemented, they may then be able to slowly chip away at the mortar of their partner's faith, change them and lead them away from the church.

This very infrequently ends up the case, though. These emotionally tortured agnostics consequently find themselves trapped in an existence of attending services and suffering through endless religious discourse and theological discussion as the only way to spend any time with their partner at all.

This domestic situation can be particularly cruel when children get involved. The youngsters may follow in the footsteps of the Angler-can parent and become indoctrinated into the church themselves. This drives a bitter and divisive wedge between child and non-Fishian parent. Alternatively, if they do not find the faith, the poor, suffering children are forced to make a heart-rending decision that should not confront any so young: either endure the endless torment of forced participation in Angler-can religious observations, or join the agnostic parent in near total estrangement from the devout parent.

Finally, there is the segment of the congregation that often forms the basis of negative stereotypes formed by those outside the flock – and presents the major source of confrontation, schism and division within it: the ultra-conservative, ultra-orthodox, fundamentalist, zealot, fanatic. Call them what you will, every church seems to have its own particular, and often peculiar, version of the firebrand fraternity. They are often perceived as sect- or cult-like, even by the moderate mainstream of their own congregation.

Suicide bombers, self-immolators, people who feel the need to murder family-planning clinic workers in order to protect the inviolable sanctity of human life – Buddhism, Hinduism, Islam and Christianity have them all. When it comes to our mate worshipping his power pole, he is simultaneously the conservative, mainstream and extreme radical fringe of his solitary religion. The internal factional confrontations that occur there must be spectacular.

Anglercism is no exception in this regard. Its own particular brand of extreme evangelist is the born-again fisho (or BAF), a creature that has come to the church late in life and now expounds the virtues of slavish devotion and adoration with a fervour that borders on fever.

Drunk with salvation, high on god and blinded by faith, the BAF exudes enlightened zeal from every spiritually awakened pore. They can be confronting and disturbing creatures, particularly to the life-long worshipper with his comparatively understated religious observances. The BAF feels a burning compulsion to shout their new-found devotion from the rooftops, turn every social conversation into a theological dissertation, preach, proselytise and browbeat into submission every heathen they can manage to entrap in their hypnotically glassy-eyed missionary stare.

There seems to be an aching need in BAFs to compensate for the previous portion of their life *not* devoted to the pursuit and worship of the mighty piscator by having every waking moment of their brave and enlightened *new* world consumed with either the act of, preparation for, or intense earnest discussion of … fishing!

The time we live in sees the gospel of Fishianity spreading like wildfire through the masses. With conversions through the power of personal testament assisted by the tireless work of TV angling evangelists, the flock of the faithful swells.

We as a denomination are fast approaching the glorious day where we shall stand tall and proud and demand our Rod-given right to celebrate holy days with appropriate religious rituals, free from persecution by intolerant employers and governments.

When the holy lunar scriptures tell us that time and tide is right to worship, we dare not risk sullying our everlasting souls by attending to such worldly temptations as work. When word spreads through the faithful of a heavenly host of the holy piscator congregating in consecrated waters, we must immediately undertake a pilgrimage to make offerings of bait and lure. We cannot be delayed by distractions such as mowing lawns or visiting in-laws.

Join with me brothers and sisters in a small 'Hail Mullet', a prayer of thanks for the bountiful grace of Fishianity as dispensed through the selfless works of the Angler-can church:

Hail cast net, full of mullet. The fisho is with thee.
Blessed art thou among baitfish, and blessed is the fruit of thy sacrifice.

Holy snapping poo-holes. What a mother of a barra.
Pray for strength of knot and leader, now and when she hits the net.
Ah-metre-ten.

Here endeth the lesson.

Millennium metrey

ANYONE WHO HAS ever wet a line generally has a one-that-got-away story. Most fishos worth their salt have a whole anthology of them. This is mine.

It is a yarn of such sensitivity that when retold or even referred to tangentially, it still gouges at raw emotional wounds over a decade later. Before I proceed any further into this haunting, heart-rending tale of struggle, loss and regret, I need to make a clear and unambiguous declaration.

My wife, Jo, is my soulmate, my best friend, my life partner. Without her I am a worthless, directionless, empty husk of a man who would live in squalor, exist on a diet of sausages and beer and wear the same clothes until the stench became such that no self-respecting camp dog would even approach me. She is the fizz in my bubbly, the spark in my plug and the catch of a lifetime. There is no word she could utter or deed that she could commit that would sway my undying devotion to her – or is there?

The events in question take place around the advent of the new millennium, the year 2000. The apocalyptic predictions associated with the dreaded Y2K bug had the world in the grip of a 'Repent for the end is nigh!' panic.

I was required on deck for the ABC in case Armageddon did indeed erupt when the clock struck twelve. Contrary to all dire predictions, a distinct fizzle was heard to ring around the planet following the dawning of 1 January 2000 as it advanced through the international time zones.

No planes fell out of the sky; no bank balances disappeared in a puff of silicone smoke; there was no second coming of the lord or first coming of the invading alien hordes. People had a few too many sherbets, blew horns, danced on tables and generally woke up in the 2000s considerably worse for wear hangover-wise, but apocalyptically unscathed.

Jo and I licked our wounds and laid low on the day of dawning of the new age, but on the second day we rose again. (Praise be to Berocca.) We decided new beginnings and a new century needed to be celebrated in the most appropriate Top End fashion, that is by going for a gentle harbour jolly.

We headed to Buffalo Creek, a Darwin suburban boat ramp that provides access to Lee Point, our planned destination. Due to the very low tide we had to drop the trailer wheels onto the rocks at the bottom of the ramp to launch our beat-up old tinny. She was not much to look at – 12 foot 8 inches in the old measure with a cantankerous, smoky, old two-stroke Johnno 25 on the back. While dented, scratched and widely patched with epoxy putty to keep her afloat, she was no stranger to having barra come over her gunwales and we loved her.

There wasn't quite enough water to get over a small rock bar just downstream from the ramp when we launched, but I knew it wouldn't be long with a 7-m high tide about to roar in. Sure enough, by the time we had organised ourselves and got the rattling two-stroke running on a relatively steady note, the first push of the incoming tide was washing over the rock bar nicely.

We motored slowly up, and after a bit of a clunk and a thump on the already heavily scarred skeg of the motor, we pushed over with ease. Another small tinny had launched just behind us with only the one bloke aboard. I gave him the thumbs-up that it was OK to proceed and got a wave of acknowledgement and thanks in reply.

It was a beautiful day. Steamy, of course, as you would expect in January, but a slight breeze wafted off the ocean which was enough to move the moist, heavy air about and provide some relief. We cracked a cool bevvy and Jo started laying out our assortment of savoury nibbles. I turned the tiller into the current and commenced our leisurely putter towards the mouth of Buff Creek and the open water beyond.

All seemed good and right in this brave new age. Though only an insignificant nanosecond in the greater time span of the Earth's existence, maybe this ticking over of the metaphorical second hand to the new millennium did indeed hold promise of a better, bolder, brighter future. Then again, maybe this boundless optimism was just due to the fact that I was now on holidays and did not have to contemplate the vile scourge of work for a couple of weeks.

I had only brought one rod and a handful of lures as it was primarily a leisure cruise. I strapped on a big seven-inch fluoro

Nilsy and lobbed it out the back to troll the mangrove line of the creek. We had only progressed about 50 m, but it was time enough to place the rod in the holder and consume a smoked oyster on a water cracker and a slice of pear smeared with blue vein cheese, when the lure was smashed with an almighty wallop.

The rod bucked violently in the holder and bent into an extreme arc that was surely approaching the load tolerance of the small bait caster. The reel peeled line in a high-pitched, tortured whine. I dropped my beer and beautifully crafted hors d'oeuvre unceremoniously onto the deck and struggled to release the loaded rod from the holder.

Once free, I ratcheted up the drag a little to try and slow the freight-train progress of my quarry, but I could tell by feel that I couldn't crank it much further or the beast would simply bust me off.

In my lackadaisical preparation, the drag had been set fairly high in the first instance, higher than I would usually allow for an untended rod on the troll. Nevertheless, this as yet unidentified creature was having absolutely no problem in treating a fair amount of handbrake as just a small inconvenience to its forward progress.

I squared myself up to the direction in which my line was rapidly disappearing and assumed the position just in time to be presented with the Top End fisho's vision splendid. An absolute behemoth of yellow-finned, chrome-plated, saltwater barramundi violently thrashing its mighty shoulders back and forth as it partially broached the surface, the sun reflecting blindingly off its expansive silver flanks.

I froze momentarily as a million synaptic sparks fired at once and created a cerebral log-jam of inactivity. My eyes goggled, my jaw dropped, the blood drained from my face. I possibly even dribbled on myself. As the fish regained the water and made a powerful beeline for the mangroves, I snapped out of my catatonia and set about stopping the brute from making the safety of cover.

'Oh, my God!' Jo muttered. My power of speech was still significantly compromised by the enormity of events and I could only stutter a series of unintelligible, unrelated syllables before finally making a mildly coherent statement. 'Um, ba, te, humba … It – it – it's the s-size of a #$%@*&# dolphin!'

The line scythed through the water parallel to the mangroves with a sibilant hiss. 'Get outta there!' I grunted through gritted teeth, leaning even harder on the rod and gently thumbing the spool. If it got in among the tangle of mangrove roots it was all over. My gamble with the breaking strain of the line and the veracity of my knots paid off as I slowly began turning the fish's head.

Next came the angler's most dreaded sensation on a rod and reel – the sudden total absence of any tension. Had I dropped it? No. I could see the slack line disappearing under the water in the opposite direction. The fish had turned and was running back behind the boat. I frantically whipped in as much slack line as I could before the strain returned and indicated the behemoth was now making a break for open water through a channel in the expansive sand bar that separates this long straight section of Buff Creek from the outside.

When the fish felt the tension re-introduced, it launched another spectacular tail walk and I could see the brightly coloured lure being shaken violently back and forth around its bucket mouth. I prayed it would hold fast. I turned towards the monster barra once again and it hurtled down the main channel of the creek.

There was a protracted session of taking three and then giving two back before I finally seemed to be tiring the big girl and gaining the upper hand. It is impossible to tell when you are running on excessive levels of adrenaline how long events actually take in these situations. While all this had been going on, however, old mate who had launched behind me had motored slowly up the inside, anchored a safe distance away, cracked a beer and settled in for the show.

I had the fish close enough to the boat now that she could see the hull. Spooked by this foreign apparition, she launched another few shorter runs. She was definitely nearing the end of her tether though and I roared at Jo, a little louder than was really required, to grab the landing net.

Jo was certainly no novice at netting barra, but my unusually aggressive manner had her a bit rattled. Neither of us had ever dealt with a fish the likes of this leviathan before. I dragged the barra close on one pass and finally got a good look at her, complete and close up. I gasped. This was not just a metrey, it was a horse, an absolute slapper, well into the 120 range!

I reverted briefly to my strange dialect of 'Um, ba, te, humba …' but then mentally slapped myself around and demanded I take a solid grasp of myself and focus on the job at hand.

With the fish mostly beaten, all that was left to do was the theoretically simple task of leading her nose-first into the net. The problem was that the net was never going to fully contain this beast. Even though she was fatigued, the sheer mass of her made manoeuvring difficult. A final unexpected violent kick was always a possibility, if not a probability.

The big, fluoro Nilsy was draped down her cheek and I shuddered as it appeared to be holding the fish by only one treble. To say the tension in the boat was palpable is something of an understatement. I tried to remain calm as I coached Jo as to which way I was going to drag the fish and when I wanted her to strike with the net. (In hindsight, this coaching may have been just a tad strident – and probably bordered on a deranged harangue.)

I lined the fish up for a sweep towards the net. Jo dropped a bit early and spooked the fish onto a short run. Second sweep. Timing was perfect, but a last-minute jink saw her unsuccessfully chasing a massive flank with the net.

I would like to think at this point I said something along the lines of, 'This time, darlin'. Don't worry!' But I don't think I did. There is a much greater likelihood that I vented a few short, sharp, high-intensity expletives. Though these would have been purely out of frustration and directed at myself, the sky and proceedings in general, it is easy to see how my beloved may have interpreted them to be cast at least partly in her direction.

I am a pretty placid bloke generally, a big softy really. This adrenaline-fuelled, mouth-foaming monster that was presenting itself to Jo was a foreign being and very disturbing to say the least.

Maybe if I had been in possession of the composure to calmly encourage her in understated tones, the fishing gods would not have ordained the next cruel sequence of events.

I dragged the fish past for the third sweep. It was close enough for me to reach out and touch. Jo stabbed the net in but mistimed her run and slammed the barra on the snout with the leading edge of the landing net. Then, in an attempt to get in front of the fish again, she dragged the net quickly forward, hooking the back treble of the lure in the mesh in the process. This change in direction of force was enough to free the front treble from the fish's cheek.

For a moment that is burnt in my memory forever, everyone froze. The magnificent behemoth of a barra just floated serenely near the surface. I stood mouth agape with the lure swinging freely from the end of my rod. Jo held the empty net partially aloft. Then, the spell was broken – the mighty barra gently turned on its tail and swam from sight.

I collapsed onto the bench seat with a resounding thud. Jo remained frozen. There was a sudden eerie silence aboard the tinny, punctuated by the seemingly contemptuous squawk of the circling seagulls. I became aware of my own rasping, exerted breath. My hands were shaking uncontrollably, my stomach churned, my heart pounded.

Finally, Jo sat down but said nothing. I retrieved the lure by hand from where it floated jauntily only a few feet away and dropped the rod into the bottom of the boat. Jo cowered at the front of the boat, staring at me transfixed as she waited for some form of reaction, anything. Would I gnash my teeth, beat at my chest and gouge at

Above: The original Tinny team after a Billabong broadcast — Rob Smith, Tim Moore and producer Morgan Hartney. (Brooke Bannister)
Below left: A Top End vision splendid — the mighty barramundi in full flight and fight. (Peter Zeroni) **Below right:** Current Tinny producer M.C. Fadge with a cracking 'skinny' (queenfish). (Peter Zeroni)

Competition action — Compain, Bartolo, Ryan and airborne barra. (Lincoln Kirby)

Shady Camp Surprise!
(Steve McEwan)

A nice cold 'traveller' with a few mates. (Aaron Geier)

A classic run-off colour change, this one on the Daly. (Glenn Dinwoodie)

Gold! Tinny boy Smith bags some sizable nuggets on a fishing trip where someone else does the steering and the cooking and the washing up for a change! (Cranky Mick)

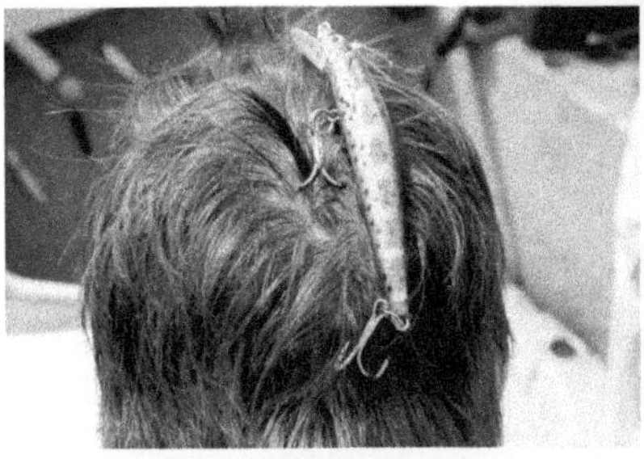

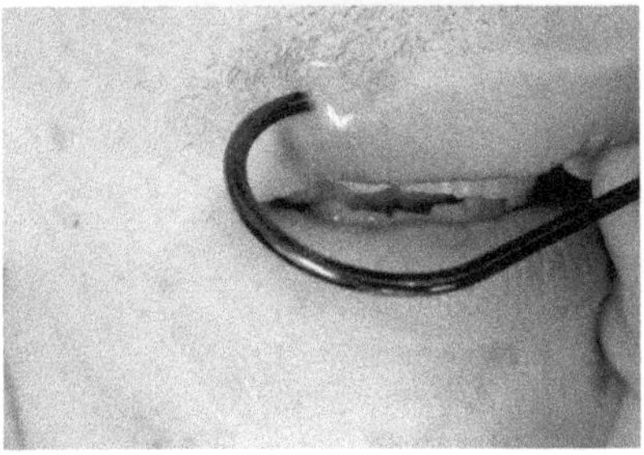

Ouch! They don't call them 'hooks' for nothing. (Jason Rogers, Evan Dixon)

Above: Young — but with attitude. Kids culvert fishing in the Top End. (Glenn Dinwoodie)
Above right: Bream fishing, Territory-style. (Jean Marc 'Frenchy' Majeaun)
Right: Yeehaaa! Chonga joins the metre club. (M.C. Fadge)

We're not the only ones who like a feed of barra. (Rikki Zulkarnain)

Above: Hail Caesar! Not sure whether the dakking was by way of prank or celebration, but a nice jewy regardless. (Steve Hunter)
Above right: Ol' macky is back in town and getting some air! (Peter Zeroni)
Right: Go girl! Michelle bags a billabong beauty. (Patty Hastwell)

Ol' Macky down below and about to get some 'pacifying'! (Evan Dixon)

Above left: Wet work. Look carefully, there are two Hiluxes in this pic. Read the chapter 'Marakai Dunk' for the full story. (Annalise Murch)
Above right: How good does it get? Early morning rock flick. (Jean Marc 'Frenchy' Majeaun)
Below: When the fishing goes a bit quiet at Cape Don, what about a spot of shark wrestling? (Steve Hunter)

Schools out. Young fellas bagging jew on the blue. (Karen Weston)

Left: Spanish sashimi. The 'men in grey suits' will always take their cut of a hooked mack if given half a chance. (Lincoln Kirby)
Right: Territory swamp person checking his cherabin pots. Note the muddy face camouflage making him invisible to crocodiles. (Aaron Geier)

Above left: Dry season? Tuna time! (Peter Zeroni)
Above right: The power of the bearded man! The Tinny firmly believes bearded men catch more fish. (Aaron Geier)
Below: Incoming! Israeli traveller Novon Mashiah was posing for a photo on a dinghy when a 4-metre salt-water crocodile leapt out of the water to try and attack him. (Doron Aviguy/Newspix)

my eyes? Would I cast myself over the side to seek a watery demise? Would I explode into a hissing, howling, spitting, roaring, whirling dervish of profanity, abuse and recrimination?

I did none of the above. I felt strangely empty … nothing. I was speechless and felt unable to form any coherent thought, comment or emotion, let alone articulate it. With a huge, melodramatic sigh I turned to the motor, pulled the rip-cord, engaged gear and motored slowly up the creek on our original heading. I recast the Nils Master out the back and settled into an assuredly futile, melancholy troll.

Jo told me later that in all our many years together, she had never felt scared of me. I have never even raised my voice to her let alone a hand – but at this particular point in time, she was terrified. My unnatural silence, the thousand-yard stare, the total lack of eye contact and reaction of any kind to what had just happened had her totally rattled. I felt physically and emotionally broken.

As we trolled past the bloke who had anchored up for the show, he looked over and shook his head in commiseration as he retrieved the anchor that had held him in place for the duration of proceedings.

'Fish of a lifetime that was, mate. Bad luck,' he muttered sympathetically.

'Thanks heaps for that,' I thought.

The significance of the metre barramundi, particularly to one who has not yet joined the club cannot be overstated. It is an emotional yearning, a visceral need, a yawning chasm of inadequacy inside you. And this fish had not been *just* a metrey, it had been a bona fide horse. It would have been the first fish of the new millennium. Poetry, fairytale and fable all rolled into one massive great big slimy silver package. But alas, it was not to be.

When the emotion of the event receded somewhat a few days later, and we were able finally to delicately discuss the affair, I told Jo, 'Don't worry, love. I'll get another one.'

To this day, that prediction has not come true. If and when it finally does, maybe then the healing can commence.

The dry

A LOT OF people absolutely rave about the dry season. They ceaselessly and repetitively wax lyrical about how unbelievably beautiful the weather is. They prance about casting flower petals from side to side, beaming like rapturous born-agains and using the word balmy far too often.

The dry is the Beer Can Regatta, the Mindil Markets and cloudless blue skies. Its onset heralds the proliferation of dragonflies, visiting relatives, backpackers and grey nomads.

Now don't get me wrong, I like a bit of dry – 'bit' being the operative word. About six weeks of dry is an eloquent sufficiency in my book. This provides just enough time to fit in a couple of nice dry-season camping trips, the Darwin Festival and the Darwin Cup Carnival. Then I reckon it's time to pull up stumps and move straight into build-up.

I am often accused of being a dry-season bah-humbugger but I can't help feeling aggrieved that my Territory is overtaken by interlopers during the dry season. The markets are full of people wearing sandals, socks and ironed shirts, cluttering up access to my usual hangover breakfast vendor. They ooh and aah and point to all the exotic strangeness on offer before moving off and finding a much-less confronting Devonshire tea somewhere.

Cars bearing strange number plates piloted by drivers wearing broad-brim hats with mesh vents on the side travel at 20 km/h below the stated speed limit, or sometimes simply at 20 km/h. They perform unpredictable manoeuvres with unfathomable intent on Darwin roads, encouraged and directed by their disembodied electronic mistresses speaking in strange, hybrid accents.

Tourist drivers negotiating an unfamiliar urban road system assisted by a sat-nav device present an equivalent threat-to-life rating as a local driver dosed to the eyelids with Humpty Doo Hydro, crystal meth and OP rum. This is particularly so if they happen to have a three-bedroom chalet on wheels hitched behind them.

I might open myself up to claims of being ageist or grey-nomadist with these remarks, which is probably fair enough, but I do consider myself to be even-handed in my vilification. I delve into xenophobia to balance the ledger: international visitors also raise my ire. Beautifully groomed Euro nuclear families in expensive mobile mega-campers often travel in convoys like covered-wagon pilgrims. They are a vigorous, invasive species that clog up our suburban intersections, choke our highways and completely dominate our dry-season campgrounds. There, I said it.

These Euro/Britz/Maui folk have a significantly different concept of personal space from that of Territorians. They have no qualms about backing in and setting up so close to your tent that you are able to hear the turgid rumblings of their chemical toilet in the middle of the night. During daylight hours you are forced to endure the sickeningly wholesome daily performances of the Von Trapp Family Reality Roadshow.

Another variant is the lower budget and age demographic that travels in either the much cheaper bongo vans liveried in contrived thematic graffiti or barely roadworthy bombs: backpackers. They are a considerably scruffier mob and spend a fair amount of time drunk. This makes them much more acceptable to Territorians – we 'get' them.

One mob we don't get, though, is the Japanese holiday hippies on a journey of self-discovery through didgeridoo and djembe. The sight of dreadlocked Nipponese in baggy cheesecloth pants and tie-died shirts busking with a didj in the streets of Darwin is somewhat surreal. Arnhem Land countrymen must groan with horror as another clapped-out '80s station wagon rolls into town with a load of rising-sun yidaki (yidaki being the proper blackfella name for didgeridoo) pilgrims on board. I reckon blackfellas should play a bit of 'good enough for the goose' and roll out the blanket in downtown Tokyo to put on haiku recitals or origami performances. It annoys me that these interlopers – regardless of their colour, age, nationality or hat preference – can cause me obstruction and annoyance as I do my local thing.

As far as I'm concerned, unless you can show the ticker and perseverance to hang around through a build-up and a wet season, you have no right whatsoever to enjoy the benefits of our dry season.

National chains still dress their shop windows and bombard our letterboxes with this year's winter fashion in an extraordinary display of one-size-fits-all mindless conformity. It's ridiculous. You do occasionally see some desperado slave to couture parading around in the latest piece of faux fur-lined fashion, but they suffer terribly for their art. It's still 30°–32° during the day, after all.

This year's winter fashion round these parts is the same as last year, and the year before, and a decade ago for that matter. Whenever the mercury plummets to an overnight minimum figure somewhere sub 20°, the next morning sees the fashionistas of the Top End shiver with horror. They wrap themselves in a doona when finally able to extricate themselves from bed and set about digging the boxes of winter woollies from the back of the cupboard.

Heading to work in the Darwin CBD on days such as this rewards one with a display of magnificently uncontrived retro couture. You are confronted with a car crash of mismatched colours and styles. Fleeting trends of bygone times that should really have stayed gone gain a brief regional resurgence. Wearers of ugh boots accessorised with stretch-denim, acid-wash jeans stride along in step with others who have simply pulled fleecy tracky-daks over the top of their usual attire. There is a passing parade of jackets, trousers and jumpers that were bought by the wearer when they were a significant number of years younger, a similar number of kilos slimmer, and apparently drunk, on drugs – or possibly all of the above.

The best part for me about this resplendent dry-season fashion display is the absolute lack of shame and self-consciousness. 'Yes, I do realise I am perpetrating heinous crimes against couture, but I am cold and I don't give a stuff!'

There is a real show-and-tell atmosphere as workers gather round the office urn first thing, the air redolent with the aroma of freshly liberated moth balls. Firstly, there are personal accounts of just how cold it was last night – 'I had to turn the fan off!' – and then the conversation moves on to compare the antiquity and provenance of the various outfits on display.

'I got this jacket in 1995 to wear to a B&S ball in Daly Waters.'

'We went skiing in Jindabyne in the '80s and I got these pants there. Look, they're lined with sheepskin!'

During the dry season, a fisho's mind turns to the billabongs. There is hardly a more epiphanous experience than nailing a big billabong barra as the sun pushes a crimson bloom over the horizon of the floodplain and countless squadrons of water birds take to the wing. The big rivers still produce fish during the dry, but with nothing like the numbers and ferocity of the build-up, wet and run-off. Harbour barramundi, salmon and skinny fish (queenies) are still a viable option, but a lot of focus on the harbour and wider waters turn to pelagic fishing. Schools of tuna and mackerel come closer to shore at this time of year and are a popular target for dry-season angling.

The dry also heralds the onset of the billfish season. Big rigs will patrol far and wide in search of sailfish and marlin. Increasingly though, the 16- to 18-foot brigade are tooling up to chase these impressive sport fish as well. We have heard quite a few reports over recent years of fishos coming to blows with a big sail or marlin that has taken a silver slice or mackerel lure. There are even incidents of them taking a chunk of dirty old pilly or a barra lure.

The dry is also fishing comp season in the Territory. These kick off right at the seasonal cusp between run-off and dry with the two premier barramundi comps on the Territory and Australian calendar. The Barra Nationals and the Barra Classic are held on the mighty Daly River every year in April and May. Some years the starts get delayed due to an excessively prolific wet season restricting access to the river. A series of hard-fought and prestigious billfish competitions also take place right across the Top End from Darwin to Gove and Groote Eylandt through the dry. Though the competitors in all these sanctioned events certainly have a good time after lines out, competition is deadly serious on the water.

There is also a very different kind of competition that flourishes across the Top End at this time of year – angling events with a much higher emphasis on the social than the competitive. The Alligator fishing club based in Jabiru is a good example of the many fishing clubs that run social comps throughout the dry. The fact that the Alligator mob bill themselves as 'the drinking club with a fishing problem' probably gives you an indication of the priorities at these type of events.

The pinnacle social events of the dry are associated with the Darwin Cup Carnival that culminates with the running of the cup itself on the first Monday in August. The dry continues right through August, but it is on the wane once 'the gallops' are run and won.

By the time September rolls around, the air is starting to get heavy and even the hardcore grey nomads that have persevered to this point pack up and begin their exodus to cooler climes. Humidity builds, clouds reappear on the horizon and the Top End girds its loins for the stifling oppression of the looming build-up.

How's ya sphincter?

THIS OUTSTANDING TALE of wet work came to us by way of a video submitted to The Tinny website. Some people might say it was dangerous, silly, skylarking boofheadedness – but we reckon it was an outstanding example of Territory can-do!

Dave, Tynan, Chris and Nick were all tied up in the maritime industry. They had become firm mates through working with each other fairly extensively over the years in various combinations of skipper and decky roles aboard different boats in and around Darwin Harbour.

Without stating who was who among the crew, two held Master 5 tickets, one was certified at Master 4, and one a deckhand working blue-water charter boats. There was obviously no shortage of boating experience among this crew, even though they had been mostly aboard much bigger vessels than The Tinny generally concerns itself with.

They kept in pretty close contact, but the complex rosters involved in working boats meant that they didn't all get together too often. Early one February, however, a comparison of rosters had revealed that all four would be off-duty on the same couple of days during the week.

This happy and quite rare circumstance demanded a catch-up and a few beers. It was unanimously decided that the obvious way to achieve these goals in the most efficient and enjoyable fashion possible was to go fishing.

A blue-water trip would have seemed just a bit too close to being on the job, so an overnighter on the Daly was settled on as the best option. Conditions on the Daly looked promising and being mid week, it would be relatively free of crowds of weekend warriors.

Normally the Top End could expect to be in the grips of some heavy monsoonal conditions at this time of year resulting in most of the big barra rivers being both inaccessible and unfishable. There had been an unseasonal absence of rain in recent weeks though, which meant that the Daly would not only be accessible by road, but possibly dropping. The accepted wisdom on the Daly is that falling river levels result in aggressively feeding barra. While not deemed to be an essential element of this particular trip, if the barra did decide to cooperate and go on the chew, it would certainly provide a welcome bonus.

The boys packed up Chris's 6-m poly boat with rods, tackle, eskies and swags and headed south from Humpty Doo on the 250 km journey to the Daly. Arriving shortly after lunch, they launched without delay and headed downstream with conditions looking quite promising.

They fished a few creeks on the way, nailed a few barra in the process, and as night fell, anchored up around Clear Creek. The plan for the evening was to toss about a few surface lures, toss around a few lies and insults, and toss down a considerable number of beers. All this tossing continued into the wee hours until the beckoning of the swag could no longer be ignored.

Next morning, they fished around a few favourite spots further downstream, continuing to add to the barra tally as they went. When the tide turned, they began leapfrogging the leading edge of the tidal push back upstream, fishing any creek mouths that looked worth a flick as they went.

By the time they made their way back to the ramp, they had boated quite a few fish for the trip and a dozen or so of the choicest specimens had found their way into the esky destined for the table. Somewhat weary from the fishing and celebrations and having successfully ticked the 'catch up and have an ale' box, they dragged the boat up onto the trailer and started the trek back towards Humpty Doo.

They had only made about 40 km back along the Daly River Road, however, when they came across a queue of 4WDs and boat trailers pulled over onto the verge in front of a very swollen creek.

Backyard Creek had been quite well behaved on the way in, but had obviously received a significant deluge somewhere in its catchment in the interim and risen quite aggressively. The boys pulled over to the roadside with the other strandees and resigned themselves to the inevitable wait for the water height to fall.

An hour and a half passed slowly, as tends to be the case when watching the kettle. The level had certainly dropped, but they couldn't be quite sure just how much. The flood-level marker was a good distance away midstream and no-one had binoculars or a rifle with a scope to actually make out what it was reading.

During that interminable 90 minutes or so of thumb twiddling, considerable tactical discussion had taken place. A well thought out plan had been formulated for a crossing attempt once the water receded to the 1.2-m mark. This was the level that Dave, as driver, decided he would be game to have a crack at.

The only section that seemed to be flowing with any force was the deepest stretch about 10 m wide and pretty much right in the middle of the crossing. The problem was, he couldn't be sure just how deep that section was.

There's a common saying in water crossings that if you can walk it, you can drive it. Now this is all well and good in theory, but in the Top End's croc-infested waterways, wading into swollen creeks is quite possibly more dangerous than the prospect of being washed off the flooded road in a vehicle.

Dave had stated quite unequivocally, 'There's no way I'm wading it!' But before the conversation had progressed much further than this – and unnoticed by the others until he was actually knee-deep in the task at hand – Tynan had taken it upon himself to do the wade.

Whether his decision was the result of a carefully calculated assessment of risk versus reward, an act of selfless bravery, or just plain, flat-out stupidity is open to debate. What is certain is that he waded out far enough to ascertain that the flow in the middle section was not too strong. He had also been able to make out the fully exposed 1.4-m reading on the flood-level marker, which indicated it was probably at about 1.3 m and still falling.

Pulling up on the other side, the occupants of the ute jumped out to greet the boat crew. Deluges of water began to drain from the interior of the ute's cabin where it had been about 150 mm deep at the height of the crisis.

There followed considerable high fives, excited yahooing and back-slapping self-congratulations on a well-formulated and successfully executed tactical plan. All this of course, heavily interspersed with frequent exuberant expletives that ended up as bleeps in the PG-rated and edited version of the video that eventually went up online on The Tinny website. The audio in this section of the piece sounded a little like morse code in the end.

In my mind, the quintessential line of the whole production is delivered by boat driver after vaulting jauntily over the gunwale down onto the bitumen. He meets ute driver by the still-draining rear tray of the vehicle and asks dryly, 'How's ya sphincter, mate?'

Fish in a barrel

Territorians are a pretty parochial lot as a rule, viewing everything and everyone from down south with a mix of pity, contempt, scorn and amusement. Territory fishos take this mindset to an extreme. We are dismissively derisive of our southern angling cousins, the soft conditions within which they operate and their piddling prey. Overcrowded, over-regulated, overfished and under-inspiring pretty much sums up our attitude. Bream, flathead, whiting, bass, hah! We would nonchalantly put a dirty great hook through the shoulder of most of the coveted and revered species of the southern angler and lob them back into the briny in hope of catching something decent.

Our fisheries are abundant and extensive, our catch a cornucopia of sporting and table delights. Snapper, trout, cod and jewfish from the depths; mackerel, tuna and trevally patrol the surface; skinny fish, salmon and mangrove jack occupy our estuaries and succulent mud crabs are prolific by pot.

The glowing icon of our angling supremacy though, the figurehead of our fishy fiefdom is, of course, the barramundi. Abundant about the rocky headlands and shorelines of our tropical coastal waters, prevalent up and down the length of our mighty rivers and plentiful in the placid waters of our picturesque billabongs, the barramundi is all-pervasive. If there is a sizeable puddle of water in the Territory, there's a fair chance it will hold barramundi. A large contributing factor to our unassailable sense of smug superiority comes down to the fact that *we've* got barramundi and *they* haven't.

As a direct result of this conviction, we are somewhat tolerant of far-north Queenslanders and Kimberley dwellers. We almost consider them quasi-Territorians. They have a similar climate and terrain, share our isolation and elusive sense of last frontierism – and they have barramundi.

Occupying pride of place at the pinnacle of barramundi-fishing achievement is the metrey. An object of desire, frustration and obsession, the metrey is held in reverential awe. Catching this benchmark in barramanship marks a rite of passage. As a result, there is a stark line of demarcation that divides the population of barra fishos – the 'haves', with a confirmed metre fish notched into their gun belt, and the 'have nots', who still strive for the grail in this most holy of quests. The 'have nots' are frustrated, unfulfilled, unworthy and insignificant. The 'haves' are enlightened, initiated, admired and virtuous. It's as simple as that.

To have caught a metrey is to be a member of a distinguished club, your credentials for inclusion forged in the gladiatorial cauldron of piscatorial battle. You have applied tactics, technique and strategy; displayed strength, valour and dedication. You have an incontrovertible right to claim metre-club inclusion – or do you?

A contentious issue has emerged over recent years with regard to metre-club membership eligibility. The debate centres on fish caught in stocked impoundments. Manton Dam, south of Darwin is a stocked impoundment and the Kimberley has a smattering as well, but the majority of these fisheries are located in central and northern Queensland.

Now the fact that a majority of these stocked dams and lakes are outside the Territory may have some bearing on them being deemed ineligible for official metrey recognition. (I refer you again to the Territory fisho's rampant parochialism.)

There is also the human desire evident since Neolithic times to gain inclusion into tribes, clubs or cliques that are perceived to be exclusive. Immediately you have managed to get yourself included though, the natural tendency is then to do your utmost to ensure all others are excluded.

Now, there is no denying that there are some absolutely stonking fish that come out of stocked dams and lakes, which some wild-fish-only advocates refer to as feedlots. The photographic and anecdotal evidence is undeniable. A lot of barra caught in these fisheries exceed 100 cm in length – but are they actually metreys in the accepted sense of the word?

We in The Tinny take the firm stance that they are not. We classify barra caught in impoundments as 'fish in a barrel'. The 100-cm+ specimens are impressive and interesting and demand attention and discussion – but they are not metreys.

Without mincing words and at significant risk of alienating a considerable proportion of my readership (please direct all complaints to Timothy Moore c/- fishing@your.abc.net.au), they are lazy bovines of fish who have never had to fight tidal or estuarine currents, have no natural predators to evade and are basically misplaced souls in an artificially benign environment.

In the wild, barra undergo sexual inversion around the 90-cm mark whereby males turn into fully functioning females between one breeding season and the next. Males need to be sexually active before being able to undergo the 'tackle change'. Because there is no access to saltwater estuaries where the barramundi naturally spawn, impoundment fish do not 'invert'.

This means you are left with a lake or dam full of fat, lazy blokes that are either sexually frustrated, biologically neutered or indulging in God knows what kind of acts of confused and unnatural fraternisation among the submerged timberwork.

Yes folks, it is sad but true. Impoundment fish know not of love. They do not know what it is to be consumed by a passion, desire and lust so all-consuming that they are driven to migrate hundreds of kilometres and run the perilous gauntlet of attack by shark, croc, dolphin or other saltwater predator – just for the opportunity to sow their wild oats in salty ocean currents.

The lack of any real predator is a significant contributory factor leading to the disproportionate number of fish in a barrel that regularly attain the leviathan proportions of 130–140 cm compared to fish in the wild. The two great motivating factors for all forms of life are the pursuit of sex and the pursuit of food. If you lock a bloke inside his house with no prospect of ever coming across a member of the fairer sex and no necessity to undertake physical activity, but unfettered access to a fully stocked fridge – I can guarantee you the result will be a big, fat, lazy boy.

Big impoundment fish also seem somewhat physically distorted, taking on a shape much closer to that of the golden perch or yellow-belly. They are big and distended around the gut region compared to wild fish.

This is not the only similarity with the yellow-belly, as fish in a barrel are inevitably swampy as all buggery in colour given their lack of access to nice clean saltwater to clean up their complexion. I'm quite sure the flavour of the fillets would be similarly swampy in nature should you decide to keep some. (Much chilli required.)

Yes, they are barramundi. Yes, they are fun to catch and demand a degree of skill and tactical thought. Yes, I would happily lock horns with one myself for a bit of fun. But The Tinny maintains the stance that they do not qualify as real metreys.

You might now be thinking that I am simply exhibiting the behavioural tendency mentioned earlier in the chapter (maintaining exclusivity in the club by blackballing the applications of others). This could not be further from the truth, because I must shamefully admit to the fact that I am not a member of that most prestigious club. I am not among the initiated, admired and esteemed. I am a 'have not' – constantly striving for the legitimacy and peer recognition that the capture of the fishy 'grail' would ensure.

This quest and my resultant failure to secure the prize has led to frustration, anxiety, hurtful ridicule and considerable questioning of self-worth over the years. Nevertheless, should I by some chance happen to find myself fishing an impoundment at some point and land a 100-cm+ fish, I would still not consider myself to have joined the club.

If asked, I would definitely say, 'I have got a hundred and something centimetre barra – but it was a fish in a barrel.' After making this declaration, I would fully expect a snort of disgust in reply and a sneeringly dismissive, 'Well that doesn't count, does it?' A statement to which I would meekly agree.

If I go into a zoo and blast a tiger, a lion, a rhino and an assortment of African plains deer, take photos of myself with rifle in hand and one leg planted cockily on the flanks of my hapless, bloodied prey, does that make me a big-game hunter? I think not. If I ring an escort agency to secure the services of a glamorous date to accompany me to a particularly pukka society function and she is charming witty and breathtakingly beautiful, a magnificent catch, all other guests at the 'do' are captivated by her grace and poise but she seems to notice no-one in the room but me, does that make me an irresistible babe magnet? I think not.

The logic of our argument is plain to see and overwhelmingly convincing. The Tinny has always held as one of its core virtues the obligation to 'call it as we see it'. Whether we see it through beer goggles, the prism of unenlightened self-interest, in 20/20 hindsight or through the tunnel vision of narrow-minded blinkers is of absolutely no consequence. In this instance, this is the way we see it.

A barramundi that is 100 cm in length or over, but procured from a stocked impoundment, cannot claim the official status of metrey. Hence, any fisherman whose only barramundi of 100 cm or more was sourced from the aforementioned environment cannot claim to be in the metre club. He or she should relinquish all claims on membership and desist from making any public statements that might lead others to believe that he or she is indeed in the club.

Harsh, yes, but fair.

Test driven to drink

MARK CALLAGHAN IS a poddy mullet who we first heard from at The Tinny a number of years ago. Now when we say poddy mullet, we are not casting aspersions on Mark's intellect or making reference to his predilection for bogan hair styling. A poddy mullet in The Tinny vernacular is someone who podcasts or downloads the show online, generally from outside the Territory; in Mark's case, Tasmania.

Mark has what you might call a fairly substantial touring rig: an old Greyhound bus customised to his purposes with a homemade 4.5-tonne, double-decker, hydraulic-lift trailer. This facilitates the towing of his run-around 4WD as well as a 3.5-m tinny and trailer.

His aim was to set off from his home base in Tassie and travel on a suck-it-and-see basis, with Darwin loosely locked in as a final destination. To keep him company on the many long highway stretches that this intrepid journey would entail, he downloaded a couple of hundred editions of *Tales from The Tinny* podcasts to his MP3 player.

We learned of this with some consternation. While pleased that he regarded what we produce each week to be worthy of stockpiling for saturation listening, we were at the same time quite concerned about Mark's mental stability.

In the first instance, what would possess someone to want to listen to interminable hours of us babbling on in our inimitable boofhead fashion? Secondly, and more importantly, we were worried about what state of mental wellbeing Mark would be in *after* having been exposed to interminable hours of us babbling on in our inimitable boofhead fashion.

Tim and I are both lucky enough to have adoring mummys who exhibit a bottomless supply of blind maternal pride, unconditional love, tolerance of our foibles and interest in our exploits. Even our dear old mums, however, and God bless them, would baulk at the prospect of incessant hours of aural exposure … to us. Let's face it, the UN banned the Yanks from doing that sort of stuff to suspected Al Qaeda terrorists! (Note to self: talk to Tim about the prospect of selling podcasts to the CIA.)

Mark, however, traipsed slowly up the coast, fishing his way towards the Territory and poddying himself mercilessly in the cabin of his bus. When we did finally meet up in person upon his arrival in Darwin, he seemed to be a good bloke and remarkably unscarred by the experience. In fact, his saturation exposure to The Tinny had left him with an extraordinarily solid grounding, certainly for a blow-in, about local fishing spots, techniques, seasons, species etc. He had become a graduate of the Tales from The Tinny Institute of Higher Learning!

Mark has been in the Top End for a couple of years now and fishing hard the whole time. Over this time, he's added a 4.1-m tinny to his 3.5-m car topper, a 4.65-m plate boat. As you might imagine, it was becoming a bit unwieldy having all these vessels cluttered around the big ex-Greyhound tourer, which was still his home.

Urgent consolidation of his collection of craft was required and he set about selling them off to partly fund the purchase of a brand new, all-purpose vessel. What he required was a good, solid, spacious boat that he could sleep in comfortably. He wanted it to be seaworthy enough to access wider blue-water destinations, but still be creek and billabong friendly.

Selecting a new boat is a very serious business. There are hull design features to consider, motor selection is critical, deck layouts and storage configurations to ponder – very important decisions that you rush at the risk of suffering years of bitter regret.

Finally, after a great deal of research on the many maritime options, he narrowed the field of contenders down to two or three probables. Now it was time for test-drives, the final critical factor that would determine the eventual winner.

He lined up probable number one for a harbour gallop. It was a 5-m model with 70 horses on the back and a layout that Mark reckoned was pretty sweet. The mechanic from the dealership was sent to play both salesman and skipper for the test-run. They launched at Darwin Harbour's East Arm ramp in the newly rigged vessel and pointed her towards open water. The trim of the boat just didn't seem right. Mark waited a polite minute or two to allow the skipper to make some adjustments, but when it appeared he seemed quite happy with the way it was travelling, Mark commented, 'Ya don't reckon the bow's riding a bit high do ya mate?'

'Yeah, the motor might be mounted a little high,' was the mechanic's response.

'Well, you mounted the bloody thing, didn't ya?' Mark countered. 'How do we find out for sure?'

'Like this!' said the 'skipper', who throttled back slightly, threw the wheel over hard and then punched it up to full revs!

The next few seconds were something of a blur. The motor roared to full throttle, the hull lurched and tipped up to 90 degrees, burying the right gunwale in the water and tossing both occupants unceremoniously into the drink.

Mark remembered being told that these new-generation motors had a cut-out switch that activated as soon as the motor sucked air, so he assumed, or more accurately hoped, that the boat would come to a halt not too far away. As he broke the surface though, he heard the motor cough, splutter and then roar back into full life as the hull righted itself and immersed the water inlets on the motor once again.

The hull now appeared to be trimmed beautifully, looking hydrodynamically correct and quite graceful in the water as it roared off into the distance at full noise. The only problem was, they were not aboard.

As the tide started to rip them out towards the middle of the harbour, Mark began to become a tad concerned. He had been out in this particular part of the East Arm just the day before and had remarked on how thick the stingers had been. He had also caught quite a few medium-size noahs here in his time and had lost hooked fish to bigger models. Then, of course, there was the ever-present threat of crocs. 'What did I do to deserve getting saddled with this dickhead?' he thought.

Both blokes drifted along in the current for a while and took stock of their fairly limited options while getting over the shock of the initial incident. The test pilot was getting a little bit panicky and bottom-lip quivery and began to dissolve into an, 'Oh my God, WE'RE GONNA DIE!' routine.

Mark told him to shut up and calm down and added: 'We're not going to die, you idiot.'

The last part was mumbled under his breath, though Mark didn't really give a rat's arse if the bloke heard him or not. He could not think of any action more worthy of having someone officially and irrevocably designated as an idiot than the test pilot's recent antics, particularly given that he, Mark, was having to live with the consequences.

'Idiot!' he said again, with more conviction this time.

He shook his head. His call of, 'Shut up, we're not gonna die!' had been purely a reaction to the test pilot's mounting hysteria and designed to stop the bloke going into a flat panic, but Mark was beginning to have serious reservations himself.

It was a quiet Friday. They hadn't seen much boat traffic about and there were bugger-all cars in the boat ramp car park so there was a low probability of boats returning this way any time soon. Mark maintained his veneer of outward calm so as not to add further fuel to the test pilot's whimpering hysterics, but he did start to think along the lines of, 'Well, I've had a good trot ...'

Meanwhile, further round East Arm, a bloke and his missus were having a quiet Friday arvo fish when they noticed a tinny heading their way going absolute flat bickie.

'That's a bit excessive,' they remarked as the boat continued in their direction.

Their concern turned to a mild panic, however, when it appeared the vessel was making no attempt to navigate around them and was not going to miss them by much, if at all. They had left it too late to start the motor and take evasive action by this time, but luckily the runaway runabout just missed them. It roared past uncomfortably close – close enough for them to be sprayed by its bow wave, and see that there was no-one aboard. Realising that there was a very good probability that an un-crewed vessel meant someone was in the drink, they upped anchor and set a course roughly on the heading from which the kamikaze cruiser had approached them.

Mark and the test pilot had been in the water about 10 minutes when a boat appeared on the horizon heading vaguely in their direction. Mark started waving his hat and splashing about in an attempt to gain their attention and ordered his 'mate' to do the same. There was a fair bit of wind chop on the surface that day, so their prospects of being noticed weren't the best. They had to make some sort of effort, though, as this might well be the only vessel in this part of the harbour. They continued waving vigorously, but their hearts sank as the boat veered off the heading that would bring it towards them and to the rescue.

It was then that the chilling thought crossed Mark's mind that maybe thrashing and splashing about might possibly draw attention from an unwelcome quarter. He did a nervous 360, looking around for any evidence of unwanted predatory company that might be in the vicinity. He slowly stopped waving, unnoticed by the mechanic, who continued his frenzied thrashing.

Mark resolved at that point that if there was any death-rolling or limb severing to take place on this day, he would do his utmost to ensure that the bloke who was responsible for landing him in this situation would be first for the jump. Harsh, but fair. Then, just as the boat was starting to disappear from sight, it suddenly veered back on a totally opposite tack. It was zigzagging in a search pattern!

With hopes raised they renewed their splashing and hat waving with some vigour, though Mark still nervously kept a wary eye on the surrounding waters. Their efforts paid dividends as the boat changed course and sped up, making a beeline directly to their position.

They were dragged gratefully aboard the rescue vessel and the test pilot slowly regained his composure as his life ceased flashing before his eyes. Mark and his 'mate' thanked their rescuers effusively. Then they thanked their lucky stars as the hubby and wife rescue team spelled out just how fortunate they had actually been …

The couple had only had their boat in the water three times in the last year. They had put in that day on a last-minute, spur-of-the-moment whim and were just about to pack it in when the unpiloted projectile nearly torpedoed them out of the water. Turning the rescue boat about, they began the journey back to where they had been previously anchored.

They didn't have to travel too far past that point before the pristine sparkling new hull and motor cowling glistened at them in the midday sun like a locator beacon, visible from a few kilometres away. Luckily, it appeared not to have taken out any other vessels on its random, jockey-less joy ride.

It was firmly beached on a mud bank but appeared relatively unscathed apart from a few scratches, and the certainty that the motor would have sucked up a gutful of mud. The rig looked passive and serene perched delicately on the bank, exhibiting no signs of the high-strung temperament that had launched them into the drink with a violent buck. The hubby and wife rescue squad nosed in to the shallows as far as they could get and the boys jumped out. Mark thought, 'I should just stay in this boat boat and leave you here on your pat, you clown.'

The mechanic retrieved his phone from the tinny. Luckily he had made a great show of stowing it in dry, secure storage at the ramp. He made the uncomfortable phone call to the boss of the dealership.

Mark couldn't stand to listen in. He assumed the tale being told was necessarily light on facts. The test pilot spent a fair bit of time not saying much except 'err, but, um …' while the boss obviously vented his spleen. Finally, he gave some details of their location before the call seemed to be cut abruptly short from the other end.

Apparently a salvage crew of boys from the shop had been despatched with another boat to assist with the refloating and recovery of the runaway tinny. There was nothing to do but wait. Mark was in no mood to make small talk about fishing or footy (or any f'ing thing to be totally honest) with his co-marooned compatriot, so he wandered off on the sand bar.

A crew of young crabbers emerged from a nearby creek mouth and after noticing their obvious predicament, approached as near as the tide would allow. 'You mob OK?' they shouted from a distance.

'Yeah,' Mark replied 'But could you spare some water?'

'No worries, mate.'

Mark waded out to the boys to retrieve some emergency fluid rations. Despite all the distractions and excitement and near-death adventures that had taken up his day thus far, Mark was at heart a fisho and couldn't help but pose the question, 'How'd ya go fellas?'

'No good,' they replied. 'A bloody great croc has been smashing our pots and chasing us off, so we gave it the arse.'

'Great,' thought Mark. 'Ten minutes ago we were splashing around in the water like wounded heifers not far from here.'

He quickly waded back to the mud bank and kept his eyes peeled. Once again he silently vowed that if one bloke was gonna get taken, it sure as hell wasn't going to be him.

Eventually the tide turned and the boys from the dealership arrived in the other boat. Between the four of them they managed to turn the tinny around and refloat it. The motor started despite having ingested a fair dose of Darwin Harbour mud and sand. Apparently, the test pilot was not game to try any more spectacular acrobatic stunts by way of a sales pitch and maintained an almost ridiculously sedate pace as they headed back to the ramp. Needless to say, the conversation was somewhat stilted on the return voyage.

Funnily enough, Mark did actually buy the boat in the end, albeit with a brand new donk. 'The mongrels didn't do me that good a deal though, even after nearly killing me!'

Italian Mafiosi are apparently of the opinion that 'Revenge is a dish best served cold.'

Maybe the telling of this yarn is your revenge, Mark. Enjoy.

The build-up

The build-up is as much a test of endurance as anything else. Tempers fray and alcohol consumption skyrockets. UFO sightings, domestic disturbances, pub brawls and road rage incidents increase exponentially. The whole community seems to operate on a slightly unhinged basis: tetchy, toey and a tad delirious.

It is alternatively known as 'mango madness', which has a nice ring of tropical frivolity to it, or 'murder season', which doesn't really evoke the sun-and-fun feel quite as well.

The humidity is constantly on the increase from late August but the build-up really hits its straps around November. Life becomes a torturous sequence of 35°+ days coupled with 28°+ overnight minimums and saturation-level humidity. The air takes on a palpable viscosity and you form your own personal puddle of perspiration if you stand in one position long enough.

There is a seasonal surge in arrests pertaining to nude drink driving. For a significant portion of the Top End population, the onset of the build-up seems to trigger primeval urges planted deep in their psyche to get on the grog, get their gear off and get behind the wheel.

Afternoon storms that hold the promise of cool respite from the endless oppressiveness dance tantalisingly around the horizon, only to disappear into the distance leaving behind a cloud of disappointment – the ultimate meteorological prick tease.

Sometimes hopes will be raised momentarily as a short, sharp, isolated daytime downpour will temporarily ease the suffering. This only lasts until the beating sun returns and with a cruel twist of the knife, vaporises the recently deposited precipitation, thereby kicking the humidity up to further seemingly impossible extremes.

An entertaining pastime at this time of year, enjoyed by smokers in particular due their banishment outside, is to watch southern or international visitors arrive at the airport. They have often travelled many hours from their point of embarkation in much cooler locales, swaddled comfortably in climate-controlled cocoons. The moment they stride through the automatic sliding doors of the airport terminal they're confronted with the steaming, full-frontal assault that is Top End build-up. It's pricelessly amusing for locals; we never tire of watching it.

They stagger as if physically punched, their faces contort in shock, surprise and distress as they desperately suck in their first few lungfuls of build-up 'soup'. Their brains frantically try to ascertain whether they are, in fact, breathing – or possibly drowning.

Then, the desperate disrobing commences, right there on the footpath. All decorum, grace and sophisticated composure is abandoned as they strive to rid themselves as quickly as possible of layer after layer of inappropriate attire. A distressed and semi-delirious muttering often accompanies this display, which can continue right down as far as boxer shorts and singlet.

The florid complexion is in stark contrast to their pasty sun-starved legs and the overall wilted and distressed appearance brings great joy to onlooking locals who chuckle to themselves and mutter, 'Get that into ya, mate!'

The build-up is a steamy, stinky, sticky trial by atmospheric oppression. It winds and winds the clock spring of the population to a point of such unbearable tension that any trivial tremor may be enough to trip the alarm and trigger an explosively clamorous bell-ringing self-detonation.

But then, after an eternity of suffering, finally, they come. A turgid black wave of impenetrable density forms on the horizon. Powerful rumblings roll together and ramp up in frequency, ferocity and volume. The inky blackness gathers momentum and begins to envelop the sky in a 180 degree arc. 'Surely this one can't miss!'

Then a euphoric anticipatory celebration erupts as the 'fridge door' sweeps through. Named for its similarity to the sensation of standing in front of a cold-room door as it is opened, the 'fridge door' effect is a comparatively icy wall of air from the heart of the imminent storm that rolls over you like a wave. It instantly drops the ambient temperature by 10° and provides the final, undeniable confirmation: 'We're gonna get it!'

Words fail to adequately describe the apocalyptic, pyrotechnic, Donner und Blitzen fury and magnificence of a tropical build-up storm. Darwin is celebrated as one of the most lightning-prone areas in the world and the undisputed, number-one destination for lightning photographers.

In 2002, an early morning squall line produced over 5 000 cloud-to-ground lightning strikes within a 60-km radius of Darwin. To put this in context, this single, fast-moving storm front produced about three times the amount of lightning that Perth experiences on average in an entire year.

The premature dark of late afternoon is split or torn apart by the incessant high-discharge strobing of lightning flash. Fearsome thunderclaps shake buildings and can be felt on a visceral level. The simultaneous blinding flash and deafening crash of a nearby strike is a seriously bowel-loosening experience. Anyone who doesn't jump, twitch or squeal when subjected to it, should, by rights, be declared clinically dead.

The fantastic fire and fury of the leading edge often only lasts for ten or fifteen minutes before the destructive front of the system rolls spectacularly on its way. Cool air and steady rain is dragged along in its wake, and a great joy is visited upon the masses.

The first serious storm to hit after a protracted build-up provokes scenes of wild impromptu celebration. The combination of air still zinging with ozone, a precipitous drop in temperature and the cleansing, refreshing, gentle rain has a liberating, intoxicating effect.

I remember during our first build-up, having endured a particularly punishing stretch of stickiness, the first relieving storm that rolled in saw my wife and me running around in our backyard in the nude banging saucepans with wooden spoons and eggflips.

We yahooed and danced about liked crazed loons in a spontaneous celebration of being freed however briefly from climatic oppression!

A fleeting moment of self-consciousness evaporated as quickly as it occurred when similar sounds of random exuberance could be heard ringing right around the suburb. We snatched a glimpse through gaps in the fence at the celebrations of our neighbours who were long-term locals, and this indicated our actions and mode of dress were of the accepted standard.

During the build-up months, barramundi are preparing for a different sort of party, but still celebrating a climatic release. The months of October and November see the biggest spring tides of the year. Barra congregate around the rock bars and smaller estuaries at the mouths of the big rivers in anticipation of getting 'on the job'.

Though they live in both fresh and salt environments, barramundi spawn can only survive in saltwater, so this is where the lovin' takes place. The large females who are the undeniable cougars of the piscatorial realm, often command the devoted attention of a number of horny young bucks. They release thousands of eggs in the slack of the big tides following the full and new moons.

One or more of the studs who have been trailing big, sexy momma in tongue-out anticipation for some time, fertilise the eggs which drift about in the tidal waters for 15 hours or so before hatching. The embryos are then washed into an ideal nearby nursery habitat, mangrove swamps and low-lying areas flooded by the seasonally big tides.

Due to this conjugal congregation, build-up barra fishing is absolutely first class, second only to the run-off in annual anticipation by Top End anglers. Also, because one's calendar is uncluttered with must-watch sporting fixtures given the brief hiatus between the recently completed footy seasons and the yet to get underway cricket season; one can devote full attention to the job at hand.

Shoal Bay, and Darwin and Bynoe harbours and the mouths of the Adelaide, East and South Alligator rivers can produce some frenetic sessions of barra fishing at this time of year. The conditions, however, are not for the faint-hearted!

It is often said that the best time to fish for barra is when the conditions are at their most punishing for humans. Being locked into a tidal creek at low water well below the mangrove level can be a test of character, fortitude, endurance and mental composure. There is no breeze or air movement of any sort, the ferocious build-up sun beats down relentlessly, and clouds of sandflies attempt to carry you away. Your clothes are drenched, your sunglasses empty and refill constantly with pools of perspiration, you marinate in a toxic cocktail of sunscreen and insect repellent. The cloying humidity is a physical presence.

It is not unknown for these conditions to tip some fishos over the edge. They will tear at their hair, gnash their teeth, foam at the mouth, speak in tongues and rip off their clothes as they leap over the gunwales in search of cooling relief in the water. Even this desperate measure is futile as the water is rarely cooler than the ambient temperature of the air, and also full of box jellyfish.

These spontaneous mental meltdowns can be somewhat confronting to other crew members, but they also present some positive outcomes. The frenzied thrashing about generates a little bit of breeze, and footage taken on mobile phones of the victim in the throes of losing it can make for a great little video production, particularly when set to a comical music backing track. This then becomes fantastic fodder for distribution among your network of mates via email or social networks.

The build-up also provides a very good window for blue-water fishing in between the east/south-easterly winds of the dry season, and the advent of the north/north-westerlies of the monsoonal onset in late December and January.

The hot, still conditions make for ideal travelling on a glassy, flat ocean. Wider reefs, shoals and drop-offs become quite accessible to smaller boats. Though wild build-up storms are a constant threat, they often tend to be tightly contained cells at this time of year. You have a good chance of dodging them on a wide-open ocean with no restrictions on which way you can run. The other side of this coin though, is that if you can't outrun it – there is absolutely nowhere to hide on that same wide-open ocean.

A lot of Darwin crews take advantage of neap tides during the build-up to load up with jerry cans of juice and undertake missions to Bathurst and Melville islands, known collectively as the Tiwis. Famed for producing top-class AFL players with names such as Long and Rioli, the Tiwis are also an absolute paradise for fishermen. The islands' estuaries and rock bars teem with barra, salmon, mangrove jack and big mobs of massive mud crabs. Inshore reefs and shoals produce fantastic pelagic action – tuna, mackerel, cobia, giant trevally and queenies (skinny fish as they are widely known in the Territory).

The deeper waters surrounding the Tiwis and the Apsley Strait that divide the two major islands produce jewies, snapper, coral trout, emperor and other reef-dwelling denizens. Billfish are also found wide of the islands. There are even a couple of fresh-water billabongs on Melville and Bathurst that produce saratoga and sooty grunter (black bream) as well as barra.

Mangrove jacks are a very common catch from the Tiwis creeks and rock bars. Though not an uncommon catch in Darwin Harbour and its surrounds, jacks seem to proliferate on the Tiwis. They are a highly prized species having cracked the trifecta of being a fine-looking fish, a fine table fish and a fantastically aggressive fighting fish.

Given the habitats in which they lurk, a hook-up is by no means a lay-down misère for boating the quarry. Their evasive prowess at running you into timber and other structures, or just burning you with pure poke, is legendary.

Buffalo, or 'Buff', Creek is an estuary behind Lee Point that is a pretty handy fishing spot in its own right. The boat ramp also provides access to the build-up barra hotspots of Shoal Bay, Cape Hotham round to Darwin's east and the nearby Lee Point shoals, a prolific producer of spaniards.

A 15-minute drive from the CBD, Buffalo Creek is almost suburban. It is the closest ramp as the crow flies to the Tiwi Islands, so is a popular jump-off point for fishos heading that way, but it also sees some reverse traffic. It's a prime spot for a leisurely land-based flick in the hope of tangling with one of the large build-up chromies that are sometimes nailed from within sight of the ramp. You might also see a 14-foot dinghy come in from the direction of the ocean. On approach, you might notice it to be carrying three or four blokes or a whole family, a number of now-empty jerry cans and sometimes, an unlucky sea turtle that happened to cross their path in transit. These will be Tiwi locals on a 100-km open-water trek to the mainland to visit relatives, bringing BBQ supplies with them!

The spectacular build-up storms continue to intermittently bring spectacular relief to the suffering masses of the Top End, until another seasonal shift is felt across the north. This new weather pattern takes hold as the monsoonal troughs begin to exert their influence, sometimes giving birth to the most violent of all storms – cyclones. It is time for the fair dinkum wet.

Raise the tinny Titanic!

MIKE, OR MUDIC to his mates, is a fisho from Palmerston. This tale of a rescued tinny begins in March 2011 after a cracking monsoonal season. A couple of Mike's mates had flown into town for a fishing safari to chase big, slapper, run-off barra. There was Luke, a Wollongong boy, and John, a Territory lad originally but now living in Singapore. All three mates had been anticipating the trip for some time and were quite excited about the fantastic run-off prospects the massive wet had laid on for them.

The original plan had been to go to the Daly, but the road in had been cut for some time and was not looking likely to be opened anywhere in the near future. With that avenue ruled out, Shady Camp and the costal creeks of Chambers Bay were settled on as an outstanding plan-B option. On the corresponding tides the previous run-off, the first new moon spring tides in March, the coastal creeks had gone barra-ballistic with a tally of something like 30+ metreys caught.

The atmosphere as the boys drove the 200-odd km to Shady Camp boat ramp was pretty buoyant. There were very confident predictions of many lineal metres of *Lates calcarifer* coming aboard. They made it to Shady without major incident and transferred gear and supplies from the ute into Mudic's 15-foot tinny, which would be their floating quarters for the next few days.

It was a pretty hefty load; enough supplies to keep the crew going for the three days they intended to be on the hunt. One esky contained the four cartons it was estimated would be consumed on the trip during daylight hours, as well as the Coke that would accompany the bourbon earmarked for evening refreshments. It was bound to be thirsty work, after all. Another large esky containing tucker was strapped in, plus extra jerry cans of fuel and all the boys' fishing gear. Needless to say, it was a little bit cluttered and cramped, but as the heavily laden vessel began the outward journey towards the open water of Chambers Bay, the boys set about lightening the load by consuming a few foamy cold ones.

They cruised the 30 or so kilometres down Tommycut Creek to the open water of Chambers Bay and then turned east towards Marsh Creek, the nominated first port of call in search of big barra. Motoring slowly up to the top reaches of the creek on the high water, the boys managed to flick up a few barra, but only of the rat variety, nothing over 50 cm. As the tide started to run, they also began moving back towards the mouth.

The short trip back out to open water, however, proved to be a little bit hairy. Manoeuvring is always difficult in a narrow creek with a strong current on your tail, and the heavily laden tinny was a bit sluggish to respond which exacerbated matters. A few incursions into vegetation resulted in John being knocked off his perch on the nose of the boat and down onto the deck by an overhanging branch on one occasion.

Once the laughter died down, John dusted himself off and bravely resumed his position up front. This time he didn't hook his legs under the bow rails as he had done before, because he had nearly got himself tangled up on his previous tumble. This proved to be a very fortunate move for John as not long after, the nose of the boat struck the submerged trunk of a fallen tree that violently slewed the boat across the creek and along the length of the submerged obstacle. They snagged perpendicular to the rapid run-off tidal flow. As the boat tipped up on its side, John read the writing on the wall and launched himself off the nose and clear of the boat.

Unfortunately, Luke, who is a big bloke at about 6 foot 3 inches and 120 kg, lost his balance and dropped to the lower side of the boat. This change in weight caused the eskies to slip down in that direction also, the lower gunwale dipped under the surface and it was all over red rover – the tinny was quickly engulfed by the fast-flowing current.

As the boat went down, Mike was already among the limbs of the fallen tree that had brought them undone having simply stepped off the sinking hull and onto a conveniently located branch. Luke was thrown into the creek, went under the hull and was washed through the branches of the tree. He re-emerged spluttering and coughing on the other side. John had managed to get a decent handhold on the bank as a result of his headlong dive and scrambled up to comparatively dry land. All three looked around, and realising the other two were OK for the moment, breathed a quick sigh of relief.

Luke had been quite on edge prior to the capsizing, having been regaled with numerous crocodile tales both tall and true from the moment his plane had hit the tarmac in Darwin. His recent near-drowning experience had forced the nightmare tales of the dreaded croc to the back of his mind and he seemed quite unconcerned about standing up to his nipples in water. When the other two boys reminded him of the strong likelihood that Mr Handbag was sure to be somewhere nearby and suggested he might like to get out of the water, his calm demeanour rapidly disintegrated into a flailing, splashing, frantic scramble to get out of the water.

He was up to his knees in silty, mangrove mud under the water and the bank above was treacherously slimy and quite steep, so all he managed to create was a very convincing impersonation of a panicked, trapped animal unable to get out of the water, ripe for a prowling predator's picking. This was not a desirable outcome.

Luckily at this point, another boat came up the creek and hauled Luke to safety. Mike's tinny was snagged firmly under the tree upside down and facing upstream. He made one attempt to get into the submerged hull to retrieve his keys, but the water pressure exerted by the tidal run made this an impossible task.

There was nothing else for it, so Mike and John joined Luke on the other boat, which then made its way back out to the mouth. There were a few other tinnys outside Marsh Creek fishing the falling tide. The crew of one of these volunteered to take the boys back to the ramp once they finished fishing. Three or four hours passed, the tide turned and the mob that had offered the lift yelled that they would be heading off in the next hour.

The boat that Mike and the boys were aboard took them back up the creek with the tide on the rise to check if the situation of their boat had changed at all. The upturned tinny had shifted a bit with the current but was still stuck fast. John got off onto the bank and Mike leapt onto the upturned tinny. The shift in weight suddenly righted the hull momentarily and Mike was able to chuck a fair bit of gear including rods up onto the bank for John to gather. Miraculously, the water pressure had held a lot of the gear inside the upturned hull, even expensive rods that had just been lying on the floor of the boat. Mike retrieved the bunch of keys, which included his car keys, from the ignition and began unlashing eskies and jerry cans to float downstream and hopefully be picked up later.

A tragedy ensued with the beer esky, however. In a cardinal sin of Territory esky etiquette, someone had left the lid unlatched after retrieving an icy-cold one before the collision. As they heaved it into the current, the lid yawned open and disgorged its precious content to the deep. The boys grieved and lamented their loss briefly, but then quickly returned to the job at hand. Recriminations and accusations would have to wait until later.

The hull remained upright for about thirty seconds before the forces exerted by the current shifted again and the boat slowly turned turtle once more. Mike helped transfer the salvaged gear to the other boat and decided to try one final look for anything further that might be rescued. Jumping back onto the upturned tinny tipped the balance of forces at play on the hull once more. As it shifted quite dramatically under his feet, Mike scrambled to the safety of a nearby branch. The tinny assumed a majestic vertical orientation and maintained it for a few seconds before spearing into the depths of the creek. All present couldn't help but notice that it was actually quite an evocative interpretation of the *Titanic*'s final moments.

Heading back out to the creek mouth again, they transferred to the homeward-bound boat. A collection of other salvaged goods was tallied up: jerry cans, tackle boxes and other bits of flotsam that had been gathered by the crews out front.

They started the journey back to Shady Camp, but hadn't progressed more than 5 or 6 km when they came across their food esky bobbing gently along in the current. It was hauled aboard and upon opening, they were presented with a beautifully iced and still well-packed tucker esky, hardly any the worse for wear! Mumbled remarks were made at this point about the probable survival of the beer esky had simple procedural imperatives been observed.

Arriving back at the ramp, they thanked their taxi and made arrangements to provide slabs of beer as fare, then drove back out to the highway and the Bark Hut Inn. Spouses were advised of developments by phone and a hire boat was organised for the next day. With logistical arrangements sorted, a large number of drinks were had.

Next morning they drove to town and loaded up with pulleys, winches and a chainsaw and headed back out to Shady Camp with the hire boat in tow. With a looming sense of deja vu, they once again made their way out to the coastal creeks.

Instead of heading straight to Marsh Creek, which had been the scene of the previous day's diabolical proceedings, they opted to go in the other direction, to Carmour Creek, which had been their intended destination for the second night in the original plan had things not been turned upside down.

Here, things did go to plan as they boated about 35 barra up to 80 cm in length. His fly-in mates may have been involved in a violent collision, capsized, catapulted into croc-infested waters and had their life flash before their eyes, but at least Mike had compensated to some degree by putting them on to some barra! As they camped in the tinny that night at Carmour, he was at peace with himself.

The next morning they motored up and into Marsh Creek on the rising tide. The hull of Mike's tinny had been secured by rope to a tree during the frenzied gear rescue, but it had somehow come unhitched in the interim and they could not see it. Even after locking themselves into the creek over the low tide, there was no sign of the stricken tinny. Despondent, defeated, but at least having caught barra, the boys called it a trip. They called it a hell of a trip actually, and headed home.

Two weeks later, on the subsequent set of spring tides, Mike borrowed a mate's boat and went out to Marsh again with a long boat hook, hoping to be able to locate the hull or snag the bow rope. His hopes were in vain. A day of prodding, probing and scooping in the area the tinny had come to grief produced nothing. Mike resigned himself to the fact that the boat probably wasn't coming back.

Fast-forward to August, a full five months later. John was back in town from Singapore for a few days and convinced Mike it was worth another crack at salvaging the tinny.

They loaded up again with winches and chainsaw and set off for Marsh Creek. As they motored slowly towards the upper reaches where they reckoned the tinny had gone down, John chainsawed a passage through the overhanging limbs and branches with considerable enthusiasm. He had grown up in Katherine and worked at a mower and chainsaw store in Darwin for a time, but was now a certified accountant pushing numbers around a screen in a glass monolith in central Singapore. He was revelling in the blokey and outdoorsy task of waving a dangerous, loud and smelly power tool about. It was so drastically removed from what had become his daily nine to five existence. He felt a surge of youthful joy at reconnecting with his inner Territory man and took to the job with a euphoric gusto – until the chainsaw coughed, spluttered and packed it in.

They were still quite a way short of where they wanted to be, so while John went about disassembling the chainsaw motor, Mike loosely tied up to an overhanging limb and dug into the esky for a couple of cold cans.

Mechanical investigations continued with limited success as the tide dropped in the creek. Mike glanced over the side and noticed a piece of rope draped over a submerged branch beside the boat. It was the same sort of rope that had been secured to his bow. He jabbed the large boat hook down into the murky drink and after not too many prods was rewarded with a resounding metallic *thunk* Further scraping and poking convinced them that purely by chance and thanks to the cantankerous chainsaw, they had tied up at the exact spot where the hull had finally settled!

Even after more extensive exploratory work with the boat hook, they still weren't quite sure of the sunken vessel's alignment, so Mike bit the bullet and jumped in to have a feel around with his feet. They had been keeping an eye on crocs in the area, and although crocs appeared a bit sluggish with the comparatively cool weather, it was still a pretty dodgy proposition. He was able to quickly and nervously fix a heavy-duty towrope round the bow rails and discern that the hull was on its side, motor upstream and nose down. With a pretty good idea of its situation, the boys nosed the borrowed boat into the bank, aligned themselves along the length of the submerged boat and hit the throttle.

The idea was to use the turbulence from the stationary tinny's prop to blast silt and mud from around the submerged hull in an attempt to reduce its dead weight. They needed to try and lessen the huge amounts of suction that would be acting on it when they tried to winch it out. They continued with this for a couple of hours until the slack of the tide, which was their cue to have a crack at raising the tinny Titanic.

The rope was fixed to a sturdy tree on the bank, the winch put into place and cranking commenced. After a considerable amount of exhaustive heaving, a series of bubbles rose to the surface indicating the seal had been cracked and movement was afoot. Hopes were buoyed – and then quickly sunk as the winch exploded spectacularly into a pile of stripped cogs and shattered casing.

A fluent stream of appropriately blue language ensued, followed by a more reasoned assessment of the situation. They tied the towrope off to the sturdy tree and left the creek on the rising tide.

During the run-off in March and April, the Chambers Bay coastal creeks sometimes resemble a Woolies' car park with the amount of boat traffic. At this time of year, however, it was unlikely anyone at all would venture up.

And so it stayed for another month. Early September saw Mike's mate John in town again, so yet another salvage mission was planned. Nothing if not persistent, these boys. This time they were loaded for bear, or croc, more accurately. Mike had fashioned a croc cage out of a sheet of heavy-duty reo mesh cut into four sections ready to be fixed together with fencing wire on site to form a 1.2-m square and 2-m high handbag hideaway. He reckoned he had rolled the dice quite enough in that croc-infested creek and everyone had to run out of luck sometime, particularly given croc activity was on the increase with the warming weather.

There wasn't even room for rods this trip after an arsenal of winches and pulleys, an assortment of ropes, a hired dredge pump and the flat-pack croc cage were loaded on board. They did manage to keep free some space for an esky full of cool refreshments, though.

So they set sail for Marsh Creek ... again. This time they launched from Leaders Creek and came at Chambers Bay from the other direction. After the ocean leg of the journey, they made their way up the creek to the still-moored tinny. The outboard-aqua-blast method was employed again for two or three hours, during which time the croc cage was assembled. They deployed it in the water surrounding the area in which Mike needed to work.

Placing the dredge pump pipes into position inside the hull proved to be a slow and cumbersome process, but finally the rig was ready to go. Mike emerged from the water with some relief. He was happy to have had his jerry-rigged croc cage to operate in, but there was no way he wanted to put the design to the acid test.

They kicked the pump into life and all went well for a good thirty seconds of gushing silty crap removal – and then the motor came to a sudden, violent, death-rattling halt. They were certainly not having a champagne run of luck with their mechanical equipment on this job. Closer inspection revealed a sizeable hole blown out the side of the block of the pump engine. Quite obviously, it would be taking no further part in proceedings. More blue language ensued.

A last-gasp plan was formulated. Mike fixed a heavy-duty, 2-tonne winch to a sturdy tree and re-entered the cage to remove the dredge gear and secure the winch rope. John assumed look-out duties and told Mike after he had surfaced from one of his dunk-and-grope-around sessions that a croc of about 3 m was over the other side of the creek showing considerable interest. Mike went down again quickly as he was very nearly done. When he resurfaced the next time, John advised him that the croc had submerged and he had lost sight of it.

As they briefly discussed this turn of events, the croc surfaced in midstream and started making a determined beeline towards Mike and the cage. John leapt into action bellowing like a banshee, hurling rocks they had stashed for just this purpose and bashing the water violently with a heavy oar. This seemed to put the croc off his run briefly and Mike launched himself out of the cage.

'That's it for swimming!' it was decided. It was all up to the big winch now. Either the boat was going to come out of the water, or the winch would pull its front end clean off. Mike had managed on the last cage run to fix the rope to a heavy-duty D-ring shackle on the winching lug of the tinny. They heaved on the winch with all their might but didn't seem to be making any progress. Then there was a tiny shift, followed by a series of bubbles hitting the surface.

They leaned into the task with renewed enthusiasm. With the suction of the mud slowly starting to release its grip on the hull, progress was made. Before long, they were able to get about a third of the boat up onto the bank.

The dead weight of the mud-filled boat became too much to drag it any further so locking off the winch and reassembling the croc cage into a shield surrounding the back of the boat, Mike and John stripped down to jocks and took turns at the back-breaking job of scooping out the masses of stinking, slimy, silted mud from inside the hull.

It was almost like an archaeological dig. All sorts of artefacts were coming out of the bog: raincoats, lures, hats. The thought that they might possibly exhume the two bottles of premium, 12-year-old bourbon that had never been accounted for drove them to greater efforts, but alas, it was not to be.

With the dredge pump on board, they hadn't bothered including other bailers or buckets so the whole task was carried out with 1.25-litre Coke bottles cut in half. Not your most efficient slush removal device. The bailing continued well into the evening, the boys covered head to toe in disgusting mangrove mud. This did give them some protection from sandfly and mosquito assault at least.

As the tide started to roll back in at about 9 pm, the call was made – Enough! The time was now or bloody never! They would push it out into the stream and if it sank again, 'The bastard can bloody well stay there!'

They pushed it out, too exhausted to really care one way or another about the result ... and it floated! Certainly low in the water and looking dodgily trimmed, but floating nonetheless!

They were almost too exhausted for a celebratory beer – almost. While John began rigging the salvaged tinny for towing, Mike removed the motor cowling. He was greeted by a perfectly formed cast in fine, silted mud, much like he had just turned out a jelly mould. He hurriedly replaced the cowl and pretended he had seen nothing.

They started the trip back out to the open water of Chambers Bay with the towed vessel handling somewhat like a dredge barge. The plan was to have a bit of a restorative kip in the mouth of the creek before proceeding. When they hit the open water though, the conditions were pristine. A slick, millpond surface shimmered off to the horizon in the moonlight, totally undisturbed by any breath of breeze. Despite their exhaustion, they realised it would be foolish to miss this opportunity and chance it turning ugly in the morning.

Leaders Creek, which had been their launch pad for this final leg of the mission, was some 60–70 km away and it would be a very uncomfortable and dangerous journey should the sea turn nasty. After considerable experimentation with trim and tilt and shifting of loads, it became obvious that there was no way they could get the borrowed tinny up on the plane with the still mud-laden vessel in tow. They resigned themselves to a very slow trip at a sizzling 8–10 km/h and settled in to make the best of it.

After a short time, Mike started to fade badly, falling asleep at the tiller. The day before the final successful salvage had been Darwin Rugby League grand final day and Palmerston, a team containing a number of his mates, had won. He had been out on the tiles till about 1 am, and had crawled out of bed considerably second hand at 5 am to load the boat and get underway.

His day since then had entailed driving, boating, winching, a near croc attack, the majority of the bailing and now at about 10.30 pm, tiller duties. He was absolutely shagged. Setting a course on the GPS and handing over to John with the direction 'just follow that arrow', he collapsed in a heap at the bottom of the boat.

Around 2 am, a change in the pitch of the motor roused him from sleep. They were near the mouth of Leaders and after negotiating some treacherous low-tide sand bars at the entrance, they motored up towards the ramp. They tied up to a tree and had an uncomfortable short nap in the unusually chilly conditions, wracked the whole time with violent, full-body shivers. Those of you outside the tropics may scoff, but the mercury probably plummeted down towards the 15° mark – conditions considered sub-arctic and life-threatening to us thin-blooded Top Enders. They seriously lamented not having the good fortune of discovering the missing bourbon in these long, cruel, cold hours before dawn.

Eventually the tide, and mercifully the sun, rose enough for them to get to the ramp. They left the salvaged tinny tied to a tree, dragged the borrowed boat out at Leaders and whipped back to town. Hitching up the long-idle, original boat trailer, they returned to retrieve their hard-fought prize.

It wasn't just a simple matter of winching the boat onto the trailer, though, of course. It weighed a ton – literally. Chris Edwards, 'The Lord of the Ramp' at Leaders, lent a hand, and after a considerable amount of heaving, grunting, pushing and pulling, they finally managed to get the boat centred on its trailer and extracted onto dry land. The trailer strained under the load of the mud-laden tinny. They towed it delicately back to town over the potholed, corrugated Gunn Point Road. Mike's boat had returned home. Exactly 6 months and 1 week after leaving.

John flew back to Singapore and Mike rested for a couple of days before beginning the laborious clean-up process. He removed all the remaining decking which was in remarkable nick considering, and blasted the stinking mangrove mud out of the hull. He pressure-cleaned the motor and then removed the spark plugs and gently hand-turned the motor to eject as much crap from the pots as possible. With the exhaust valves open he flushed them gently with the garden hose. The carburettor was taken apart, cleaned and reassembled. This process took a number of days with protracted oil soakings taking place after every procedure. Mike wasn't a mechanic and had gone about as far as he could at this point. The moment of truth had arrived.

He put new spark plugs in, dribbled a bit of juice into the cylinders and, hoping against hope, tried to turn it over. Nothing. Not a sign of life. Disappointed but hardly surprised, he resigned himself to scrapping the motor. He consoled himself that he had got the hull back, and really – would you actually expect a motor immersed in predominately saltwater for over 6 months to function?

A couple of days later as he drove home from work, however, he had a blinding, inspirational 'Hey, bloody-hang-on!' moment. He remembered during the bailing before even floating the boat, that he had unearthed the emergency cut-out clip on its stretchy lead. It had never been replaced!

With faint hope reinstated, he raced home, found and reaffixed the clip, re-primed the cylinders and with fingers crossed, turned it over. It coughed, spluttered and then eventually roared into life!

Admittedly, it was running like a hairy goat, but it was running! Mike whooped triumphantly and shut it down fairly quickly in case it might cause itself some damage. The next day he took it off to a marine mechanic who tuned the carby, did a bit more cleaning and fiddling, conducted compression tests which were all A-OK, and pronounced it good to go!

Mike had bought another motor in the interim but has now sold it on, preferring to keep the miracle motor. The hull got a clean, polish and repaint. All the remaining decking was miraculously OK after drying out so he replaced the missing segments, rewired it and there ya go – an almost new boat!

The moral of the story? I don't really know. Persistence pays? What goes down, must come up? What I do know is that Mike has a boat and motor that has a story attached to it like no other. Now do you think the boat deserves a name after that? Of course it does.

What about The *Tinny-tanic*?

Number six on the nose

Darwin Harbour is a working port and a naval base. Consequently, it has a number of shipping channels and associated navigation markers. They come in very handy as visual navigation aids for the tinny brigade as well – useful for marking favourite fishing spots.

GPSs tend to make this sort of course setting and spot marking a bit redundant these days, but you will still hear conversations along the lines of, 'Line up the red nav buoy off Larrakeyah with the Travelodge Hotel, about 2 km into the harbour along that heading you'll see a reef come up on your sounder.'

The most prominent Darwin Harbour navigation buoy in angling circles is the 'number six'. Its official purpose is to mark the start of the compulsory pilotage area for commercial shipping and it is situated between East Point and West Point, thereby marking the narrowest part of the harbour entrance.

This is all irrelevant to fishos though, who take note of it primarily because of the many bommies and stretches of rubbly bottom that surround it. Favourite waypoints out near number six consistently produce good snapper and jewies. In the dry season, when pelagics become more prevalent in the harbour, it is also a renowned hotspot for nailing seriously big spaniards – spanish mackerel.

This particular yarn revolves around 'nailing it at number six', but not in the generally accepted interpretation of the phrase.

Frank Rodriguez is a bit of a gun fisho around town. One of his mates described him to me as 'catching more barra with a rod and reel than the Ilic brothers [well-known Darwin pro-fishers] catch in nets.'

Now that may well be a slight exaggeration, but let's take it as read that he's certainly no mug. Frank doesn't exclusively devote his attention to barra, being a keen blue-water fisherman as well. This tale from out of the tinny involves one such sortie.

It was a Monday night in November a few years ago, the first Monday in November, in fact. Frank was keen on the idea of a night fish at a few favourite waypoints out near the harbour mouth, chasing jewies and snapper.

Conditions are quite conducive for a night fish at this time of year. You don't have to endure the punishing build-up sun and generally, benign wind conditions prevail. There is the ever-present chance of getting pounded by a tropical storm, but the probability is manageably low at this stage of the build-up and you can see them coming for miles on the open water.

Given it was a school night, he was also confident he wouldn't have to jostle with other boats for his pick of the marks. Despite all these positives, however, he couldn't seem to interest any of his usual Gilligans in joining him on this particular trip.

Frank ran a very sturdy 7-m ocean-capable vessel in which he had done many solo trips before. So, unperturbed, but determined to make his mates regret passing up the opportunity, he headed out alone. The plan was to anchor up on his favourite spot just before the top of the tide and fish up and over the turn, and then a few hours of the run-out.

This tactic had been fairly reliable in the past and turned out to be a pretty good option on this occasion once again. It wasn't a dynamite session, but Frank managed to get a couple of good-size snapper into the esky.

As it approached midnight the fishing slowed, so Frank decided to call it a trip and head back in before the bottom of the tide. The night was very dark. The moon was not due up until 3 am and cloud cover obscured any stars, but the GPS/chart plotter showed the way for Frank as he motored back into the harbour.

Scanning around as he approached the point where his chart plotter told him number six should be, Frank could see nothing at all. He assumed it must have been taken in for maintenance as it would be very dangerous to have a buoy of that size moored in the shipping lane unlit. Unfortunately though, that was, in fact, the case. Moments later, and to Frank's horror, he suddenly saw number six materialise out of the gloom dead ahead. With a closing speed of about 20 knots, he had no time to react, the boat smacked head-on into the sizeable chunk of floating steel and concrete with a resounding impact, and Frank was catapulted violently out of the boat and into the oily blackness of Darwin Harbour.

As he surfaced, he heard his boat continue off into the night and realised he was a long way from land without a life jacket – not the best of circumstances. After performing a quick medical self-assessment, he found that he was physically unscathed, which was obviously a significant positive.

While he considered his next move, he began to notice the sound of a motor – his motor, idling somewhere just outside his vision. It continued to build and wane in volume and after a while, Frank realised that his boat must be describing a slow arc around his position. As he was launched out of the vessel after the collision, he must have knocked the throttle back to idle and the wheel had ended up locked into a loose turn.

He tried to interpret from the sound of the motor where it came closest to him on its loop and then started swimming towards what he hoped would be an intercept point. His estimate was good and he managed to cross paths with the circling tinny. Each time it idled past he made a grappling attempt to climb aboard. However, the boat had no grab points on its exterior and after an hour and a half or so of failed attempts, Frank reluctantly gave up on trying to reboard the boat. It appeared the only result he was going to produce from persevering was to get himself wounded by the propeller.

The tide had slowed right down by this point and while the water was slack, Frank decided to make as much headway swimming as he could. He still felt relatively unfatigued and was determined to keep calm and avoid panic. He struck out towards the Darwin side of the harbour with the reasoning that there was a much greater likelihood of coming across other marine traffic in that direction.

Pushing all thoughts of sharks and other worries to the back of his mind, he focused on just completing one stroke after the next. He adopted a steady and relaxed pace that he thought he would be able to maintain for a couple of hours, and seemed to be making quite good progress.

As he pushed through a current line carrying some floating debris, he got a jellyfish sting on one arm. A short while later, he received another on his shoulder and neck. This was going to be the major danger, he realised. Should he cramp up or suffer breathing difficulties as a result of stingers, he would be in serious trouble. Land was still a very long way off, but Frank saw a small beacon blinking yellow. It appeared to be quite close, so he abandoned the attempt to make shore and struck out for the closer buoy.

A short time later he was able to clamber aboard the comparatively small harbour marker. For the next two and a half hours, he heard his boat continuing to do lappies around his position in ever-increasing circles. He was reassured by the thought that the boat would eventually hit land somewhere – somewhere inhabited, hopefully. Then come daylight, it would be seen by someone who would surely raise the alarm. Frank made himself as comfortable as possible on the structure of the guano-encrusted buoy and settled in for what might possibly be a long wait.

The pilotless vessel continued on its spiralling path through the early hours of the morning until it fulfilled Frank's wish and ran aground somewhere populated – coming to rest on the rock wall protecting the naval patrol-boat base in Larrakeyah, close to the Darwin CBD.

The abandoned tinny came to the attention of naval sentries at first light and once they ascertained it wasn't some sort of maritime terrorist assault that had come unstuck, they went aboard to investigate. The epicentre of the spiral depicted on the boat's chart plotter gave them a fairly good indicator of the probable spot where the former occupant had disembarked. The despatched rescue vessel initiated its search at this point and before long, about eight hours after his high-impact interlude with number six, Frank was spotted and picked up from his overnight camp spot.

He had lost a couple of rods and an esky full of snapper, copped a few box-jelly stings and endured a fairly harrowing experience, but his boat was relatively unscathed and he was alive!

All in all, Frank had been incredibly fortunate. When we spoke to him, he was still thanking his lucky stars. 'Yeah, no life jacket and no kill lanyard on, but I got away with it. I've only ever put the lanyard on once before, when I was fishing off Maningrida a few yeas ago, but I reckon I've changed my tune now.'

The emergency cut-out or 'kill' lanyard is a clip that attaches to your pants or wrist and has a coiled elastic cord that connects to another clip attached to the outboard. If the motor end of the clip is removed, the engine dies immediately. It's a safety measure so if you fall overboard, the clip stays attached to you but disconnects from the motor and shuts it down. A very clever technical innovation – but just about universally ignored or circumvented by Territory fishos.

As you might expect, Frank's mates were all very sympathetic and supportive given his most frightening and dangerous experience. (Yeah, right!) They unleashed a barrage of jokes at his expense, mostly variations on the very productive theme of 'Frank sleeps with buoys'.

You may remember that at the start of this tale I mentioned it was the first Monday in November, and a couple of years ago, 2007, in fact. Following on from that, you will be able to work out that he returned safe and sound to dry land on the first Tuesday in November. We asked him whether he bought himself a lotto ticket. 'No, but when I told the old man, he reckoned there had to be a Melbourne Cup omen in it.'

'Efficient' won the cup that year wearing the number six. What buoy had Frank hit? Number six. Where had he hit it? On the nose.

The Rodriguez mob was very fortunate in more ways than one that fateful day!

Illegal aliens

The Northern Territory is widely considered to be the UFO capital of Australia, if not the world. Wycliffe Well, a small Stuart Highway township, is the undisputed epicentre of extra-terrestrial activity in the Territory, a veritable revolving door of other-worldly visitors. Ranked fifth in the world for UFO activity by the *Sun Herald* in 2002, sightings in Wycliffe Well are so common that the locals claim that if you stay up all night, you will be unlucky *not* to see something.

Situated about 400 km up The Track from Alice Springs, the roadhouse boasts statues of aliens and murals featuring extra-terrestrial encounters. There are walls plastered with hundreds of UFO-related newspaper clippings and a register resides on the bar for human visitors to record their own UFO sightings.

Local Aboriginal folklore tells of visitors from the sky and many reports to this day come from the Indigenous community. Whitefella sightings stretch back as far as those recorded by troops stationed in the area during World War Two when Wycliffe Well was a staging post and market garden supplying the northern frontier.

Sceptics claim that a direct correlation can be drawn between the number of sightings in the region and the excessive amount of alcohol and possibly other substances consumed. Some harsher critics even call for mandatory DNA swabbing of the region, claiming that the only presentation of creatures bordering on what might actually be classified as alien, is the locals themselves!

While these doubting Thomases are entitled to their cynical opinions, the *NT News* is firmly behind the UFO–Wycliffe Well connection and trumpets incident after incident from its front page.

This is good enough for me. Proof right in front of your eyes in black and white! Newspapers don't lie, and the *NT News* occupies pride of place at the absolute pinnacle of accurate, factual, non-sensational print journalism. Having stated that, it must be admitted that the detail does tend to get somewhat scanty and tenuous in the main body of the story underneath the bold headline claim. I attribute this phenomenon to the actual spinner of the yarn having undergone the ubiquitous post-probe brainwashing and memory-altering procedures for which our alien friends are well renowned.

We in the NT are somewhat in the enlightened avant-garde in the Australian UFO debate. Under the guidance and stewardship of the *NT News*, we have accepted the undeniable scientific proof put forward by such reputable sources as the patrons and publican of the Wycliffe Well Roadhouse.

We believe! While down south, UFO sceptics and outright UFO deniers debate the very existence of aliens and squabble over the science, we have moved on to formulating contingency plans for the inevitable. Contact we have had in spades, so the next phase? Capture! The first conundrum that presents itself when we inevitably capture our first batch of illegal extra-terrestrial aliens is the question of where they should be processed.

Onshore versus offshore is an irrelevant concept, we are not at the technical stage of having an off-planet facility as a viable option just yet. The Northern Territory chief minister of the time, in concert with the publican at Wycliffe Well, would mount a very strong case to the international community that the town is in fact the lay-down misère, no brainer, obvious first-choice locale for an extra-terrestrial detention facility. It is almost a statistical certainty that this initial apprehension will take place in Wycliffe Well or thereabouts, so there is an obvious efficiency dividend in not having to relocate the detainees vast distances.

Given the area's long and successful history interacting with the aliens on a regular basis, there will only be a negligible, not-in-my-backyard reaction from the locals – the visitors have been in and out of their backyards mostly unnoticed for generations.

There is plenty of crown land available for the development of a state-of-the-art, best-practice, dual-function detention and scientific research centre. Needless to say, the local economy would benefit immensely from the cash flow generated in the construction phase. When complete, the influx of workers required to run and maintain the facility would guarantee the tap of prosperity would remain a gusher.

A tourist and caravan park complex could also be incorporated to capitalise on the projected boom in tourist numbers. Regularly scheduled tours of the facility allowing paying customers to gawp, point at and take pictures of the inmates would quickly become a must-do inclusion on the grey-nomad pilgrimage route.

The potential for merchandising is simply astronomical (pun intended). Tea towels, printed T-shirts, engraved pewter mugs, stubby coolers crafted from the hi-tech 'skin' salvaged from crashed UFO craft – the gift-shop takings and entry fees alone would substantially defray operational costs.

Demand by visiting overseas scientific missions may lead to the establishment of an international airport, which would in turn demand the construction of a casino, multiplex cinema and duty-free shopping precinct. Wycliffe Well's streets would be paved with alien-attributed gold!

This project cannot be viewed solely through a financial prism though, no matter how enticing that view may be. There are sociological, ethical and legal aspects that must also be taken into consideration.

The operational conditions and guidelines under which the facility could operate would have to be carefully and painstakingly formulated. There are many issues that have not been closely encountered for a first, let alone a third kind, in our relatively short planetary history.

For example, the inmates quite obviously have no human rights as such that could be either upheld or infringed – we have to ensure that our standards of detainee treatment would be found acceptable in a court of intergalactic law should one ever subpoena us.

How would we determine which aliens are children, and therefore deemed inappropriate for detention in such a facility?

How do we identify aliens that are genuine asylum seekers who will suffer severe persecution if forcibly repatriated to their home solar system?

How do we discern which are here purely for financial gain or as a lifestyle choice, a kind of mid-life planet change? How do we weed out those who actually plan to totally obliterate the human race and achieve world domination immediately upon obtaining a visa and being released from detention? A great deal of considered thought needs to be devoted to these aspects of 'Operation Alien' as well.

Very quickly, of course, an Alien Rights movement will spring up, advocating all manner of goodwill and humanitarian gestures be made to our visitors. Support networks will be set up to extend the hand of friendship, volunteers will instigate a visitors' program on a rota basis, calls will be made for the establishment of a charter of alien rights. Access to health and legal services, yoga, macramé and pottery classes, eligibility for social service benefits, all will be campaigned for as the good, fair and decent thing to do.

Community detention will be the inevitable next point of natural progression on the pro-visitor agenda. If deemed as non-threatening, why shouldn't our guests be housed in the community until their claims for intergalactic asylum can be assessed? Halfway houses could be established in the suburbs so family groups of detainees could feel they are almost part of the community, thereby breaking down the barriers of fear, suspicion and animosity fuelled by decades of xenophobic sci-fi films.

They are, after all, just like us, really. Even though they smell like a putrid blend of sulphur, ozone and wet dog and drink hydraulic fluid like free beer on a hot day. Regardless of the fact that they suckle their children in public with an acid-based gruel expressed from the tip of their spindly elongated fingers and have the ability to weld steel at thirty paces with an angry glare. Put to one side the fact they communicate in an horrendous, high-decibel cacophonous screech that sounds like fingernails being dragged down satan's blackboard and sends dogs yelping tail between legs and kills cats and budgies outright. Apart from all that, they are just like us!

In response to the Alien Rights lobby, an equally vociferous, 'Aliens Out!' opposition group will spring up. They will stridently oppose every policy, aim and recommendation of the pro-alien lobby and thereby maintain nature's natural balance in matters of this sort. The 'Aliens Out' mob will clamour loudly that *any* alien integration will lead to social mayhem.

'We don't want their sort round here! What happens when our kids start getting experimentally probed by the innocent but inquisitive offspring of the visitors at the newly integrated co-species kindergarten?'

'Who will pay for the forced repatriations if and when asylum claims are unsuccessful?'

'What happens when my rebellious teenage daughter falls pregnant to one of them just to spite me?'

As you can see, the future is fraught with confrontation if we allow ourselves to drift into this inevitable circumstance unprepared. I am not advocating either side of this argument. My wish is that we simply rise above the petty, self-centred, local planet squabbles that consume us at present, and prepare ourselves for the longer game.

A word to the wise, though, strictly on the down low. Smart money will be buying up real estate round Wycliffe Well … (knowing tap of forefinger on side of nose) … do yourself a favour!

The demise of the 15-foot snapper tinny

When thinking of fishing the Territory, the mighty barramundi generally looms large in people's consciousness, and rightly so. It is a magnificent sport fish and worthy of its iconic status, but its high media profile does tend to have the effect of sucking the oxygen of awareness from another fine fishery that we are blessed with in the NT. Fishing the deep, wide blue, the briny, bottom bouncing.

The Top End's various harbours and off-shore fishing grounds produce a bounty of tropical blue-water species. There is the black jewfish that is capable of pulling a 15-foot tinny along at a rate approaching planing speed. Magnificent coral trout and red emperor are premier table fish and are highly sought-after prizes. The explosively powerful spanish mackerel is a dynamic fighting fish and not too bad on the chew either. Giant trevally that are a prized catch down south, are regarded in the Territory as good sport at best and annoying pests at worst.

Then there is my personal favourite, *Lutjanus johnii.* Golden snapper. Goldies. A name whispered with reverential awe. I love goldies. I love chasing them, I love catching them and I love eating them. One of the great joys of Top End fishing in my book is the moment, after a protracted battle with some as yet undefined creature dragged up from 20–30 m below, that you finally see an identifiable flash of gold–bronze, slightly tinted by the jade of the briny in between and yell, 'Colour!'

Wrecks and bommies in Darwin and other Top-End harbours hold schools of goldies. Pan-size specimens are often caught around estuarine rock bars alongside their kissing cousin the mangrove jack.

They will take live or dead bait and are also not averse to smashing a lure. Heading wider, 30–50 km offshore, reefs both natural and artificial will produce the larger variety of these top-shelf chewers. A 2–3-kg goldy is a pretty good get from these grounds and coming back to the ramp with a regulation bag limit filling the esky never fails to instil a sense of pride, self-worth and hunter–gatherer accomplishment.

Among my fisho circle of mates, however, there had always been a burning desire to tangle with the monster nugget of gold, the much fabled and photographed XOS 5–10-kg variety.

These cracking specimens are catchable closer inshore around the Arnhem Land coast and other more remote parts of the Territory. From Darwin though, we needed to go wide, if we wanted to tangle with this calibre of goldy – much wider than our 15- and 16-footers could take us, even if packed to the gunwales with jerry cans.

After years of, 'Yeah, we should ...' and ' Why don't we ...', we finally actually locked in and committed to a once-in-a-lifetime, two-night charter on a fair dinkum boat. We were keen to have an extended crack at some quality fish. Another very alluring aspect of this kind of trip is that as a paying customer, you get to sit with a cold drink in hand and watch some other bugger pull anchor. The wearisome tasks of tying paternosters, replacing smashed rigs, even baiting hooks would also be performed by that very same 'some other bugger'. He would cook our tucker, make us a cuppa in the morning and possibly even tuck us into bed! What a good bugger that 'some other bugger' promised to be!

And so it came to be that late one hot, still, build-up afternoon in November, a gathering of gentlemen shuffled, twitched and paced dockside at Darwin's Cullen Bay with barely constrained nervous energy. A sense of giddy schoolboy excitement gripped us that threatened to bubble to the surface and shatter our contrived composure. With the womenfolk still about, however, we maintained an aloof, disinterested, outward cool.

The long-awaited day had finally arrived. A set of tides circled on the calendar many months before was at that very moment building outside Cullen Bay lock to a point that would allow us to finally embark upon our feverishly anticipated, 'Big Trip Wide'.

An observant onlooker to the gathering may have remarked upon the many parallels with the *Ballad of Gilligan's Island.* It proved to be a fateful trip that started from this tropic port. The mate was a mighty sailing man, Anthony (a.k.a. some other bugger), and we had a skipper brave and sure, Sean (Fish Darwin) Uden. Six passengers set sail that day ... but that's about where the similarities end.

There were no millionaires or movie stars aboard, and certainly no professors. It would be fair enough to say, however, that we did have a full complement of Gilligans.

We bade farewell to the fairer sexes and lugged our gear down the finger and onto the boat. We took a moment to familiarise ourselves with our home for the next couple of days. The *Northern Exile* was a 46-foot west coaster. Originally designed to operate as a crayfish boat off the Western Australian coast, her wide-open, covered back deck made her ideal for conversion to a blue-water charter boat for Territory waters.

Skipper Sean's plan, democratically endorsed by the punters, was to motor all night in an attempt to reach emperor and trout grounds to the north-west of Melville Island, with a short drop for the change of the tide between the Tiwis. The crew set course and settled in for a night of steaming. The Gilligans set about vigorously lightening the dangerously overstocked esky, the excessive weight of which would surely only hinder the vessel's progress.

Come 9.30 pm, invigorated by the salty ocean air, several beers and a good feed knocked up by decky Ant, we were primed and ready for battle. The tide was on the turn as we pulled up on a mark and anchored. Sean yelled, 'Drop 'em, boys!' from the wheelhouse and time passed. To be precise, the time it takes for a snapper lead to hit bottom in 25 m of water. Then absolute pandemonium broke loose!

Every bait was smashed and three of us hooked up almost simultaneously. Drags squealed, ratchets ground and a tsunami of exhilarated excitement swept over us. After a determined struggle, the first fish finally succumbed and was dragged aboard, followed shortly after by numbers two and three. It was then we began to realise we had hit the jackpot.

There is always a period of reservation between the hook-up of a good fish and actually sighting it. Getting yourself a little bit too worked up during battle only to be presented at the conclusion of hostilities with a noah or a pesky trevally can be a little deflating. This was not to be the case in this instance, though. They were goldies, and absolute stonkers!

All three were in the 60–65 cm range and probably about the 5-kg mark. These were fish that we could only dream about nailing in our usual inshore goldy haunts. You might be lucky enough to snag a fish like this once in a blue moon, but to have three come up as a first catch within minutes of our leads hitting bottom had our jaws dropping. Figuratively speaking, of course, there was no time for such pointless time-wasting exercises as jaw dropping. Jaws were either firmly clenched or intimately involved in articulating commentary along the lines of, 'Would you have a look at the size of those #$@%#@ goldies!'

The boys who had been smashed and baited on the first drop had feverishly retrieved their lines as those who had hooked up fought the first round of goldies. After quickly rebaiting and re-dropping, most of them were now onto their first fish as well. The hook-ups continued steadily and the goldies coming aboard were increasing in size. Then, just to add a bit of variety to proceedings, jewies joined in the fray. These freight trains of fish can really put up a show. It was a testament to the size and vigour of the goldies we were onto that it was hard to make a call as to what you had on until you actually sighted colour.

An adrenaline-fuelled clamour rang out across the ocean from the aft portion of the *Northern Exile* – six blokes whooping and howling and grunting with exertion, the peel of braid being stripped at pace from multiple reels, big fish slapping around at our feet. It was a raucous, but very sweet symphony.

As the tide started to rip and it became impossible to hold bottom, we hauled in line and anchor, and Sean reset a course for overnight steaming to wider fields. A quick, turn-of-the-tide 20-minute session had produced three jewies up to 110 cm, and about a dozen snapper – the biggest at 80 cm and pushing over the 7-kg mark.

We were drunk with exhilaration and exertion and, well, just plain drunk. A cracking session had produced the fish we desperately hoped we would tangle with at some stage on the trip – but on the first drop! To say we were suitably pleased with proceedings is something of an understatement. A smug, satisfied euphoria settled upon us.

Some of the crew began reliving the battle while at the same time relieving ballast from the esky. They appeared to be digging in for what promised to be a protracted and exacting dissection and analysis of what had just occurred. Then, undoubtedly, the conversation would turn to other weighty matters.

A couple of Gilligans (including myself) ignored the barrage of abusive taunts and the questioning of our sexuality to choose the tactical ploy of grabbing a bit of shut-eye in the air-con in order to gird the loins for battle the following morning.

Though bone tired, I had trouble getting to sleep at first. The events of the evening just gone, and my feverishly heightened expectations of what might yet eventuate, had my mind racing. The gentle rocking motion of the boat making its way wider still through benign ocean waters soon did the job though and I was heavily on the nod.

We woke to an ocean as flat as a biscuit, a millpond, a textbook glass-off. The air was already redolent with the aroma of hissing bacon and eggs as we emerged from our swags to be delivered a steaming, fresh brew. We cupped the warm revitalising elixir in our hands and surveyed our surroundings.

No-one mentioned anything then, or since for that matter, but I am convinced we had a simultaneous emotional 'moment'. The sea stretched off to an almost imperceptible horizon that appeared to blend into the serene blue of the early morning sky. The sunrise reflected a magnificent golden blaze across the waters, surely a promising omen for bagging big mobs of golden fish! The serenity of our isolation was almost haunting.

'How good does it get?' I muttered under my breath to no-one in particular.

But then, the idyllic tranquillity was cruelly shattered.

One Gilligan staggered to the back deck appearing somewhat less enamoured of the prevalent waft of greasy bacon and eggs and taking no notice at all of the breathtaking panoramic splendour of his surrounds. This bloke had removed a considerable amount of ballast from the esky the night before and proceeded without delay to loudly and violently remove a considerable amount of ballast from his digestive system.

There was much encouragement and appreciative applause for his efforts and some helpful suggestions were contributed with regard technique. The slightly green Gilligan wore all this with a stoic resolve while he worked towards the conclusion of his virtuoso vomiting performance. Then, looking more miserable than three sad bastards combined, and with a fairly feeble two-finger salute over his slumped shoulders to the gathered audience, he headed back for a spot of self-contemplation and wound-licking in his air-conditioned bunk. You do sometimes get that on the big jobs.

We worked the grounds wide of the Tiwis for the morning and got a few trout, cod, mackerel and threw back big mobs of trickys up to the 2-kg mark. Tricky snapper, known elsewhere as sweetlip, are very good chewing and we would normally be extremely happy about bagging a feed of them in the harbour. Our bar had been significantly raised due to recent events, however, and we were becoming quite picky.

Trickys also have a very good survival rate from barotrauma so this made them better candidates to release. Barotrauma is a condition resulting from rapid changes in barometric pressure experienced by fish dragged up quickly from the depths. The most obvious symptom of this condition is an inflated swim bladder protruding from the mouth of the fish when it surfaces. Research has shown that barotrauma is fatal to a lot of fish, including jewies, when taken from water deeper than 10 or 15 m. This is why when you reach your bag limit in deep waters, you should pull lines. Any further fish caught, even with release in mind, probably won't survive the experience.

A constant procession of giant trevally provided sport on both bait and light jigging gear, and then a cracking 1.3-m spaniard smashed a floating live bait. Spaniards really are the Exocet missile of the ocean. Sleek, lightning fast and amazingly powerful. You will not last a second on a big spaniard without heavy wire trace, and even with one, there is still no guarantee that they won't chew it through. They have amazing stamina and strength and even when gaffed and dragged aboard, still pose a considerable threat.

They thrash violently around, determined to put their razor-sharp teeth to use in a final act of retribution. Many fishos in the Top End bear the scars of tangling with a boated spaniard. Consequently, mackerel dongers (variations on the theme of a cut-down baseball bat) are always kept handy and deployed quickly and violently as soon as mister mack comes on board.

This was all good fun, but the targeted emperors and bigger trout continued to elude us. When the noahs and stargazers started to come aboard in numbers, the shame became too much for Skipper Sean and he called, 'Enough!'

Various options were put on the table. Continue our so-far fruitless chase round wider shoals for emperor, concentrate on big pelagics (spaniards in particular or possibly even a sailfish), or head back to goldy and jewie grounds. The response from the gathered Gilligans was a resounding, 'Go for gold!'

A course was set for some marks that Sean had in mind around Rocky Point on Melville Island's western tip. We would steam most of the arvo to get there and then have a few drops during the night. This was the cue for a nap for some – others continued their marathon hardcore regime and took the opportunity to renew their assault on the esky.

On arrival, an early evening drop instantly conformed to the pattern established on the very first drop of the trip. Absolute bedlam! The second our leads hit bottom, big goldies and jewies went the tonk, and continued to do so until once again the run of the tide had us struggling to hold bottom.

The aft deck of the *Northern Exile* was again littered with cracking fish, abandoned during the heat of battle to be dealt with later. We were forced to start counting fish and a new mission presented itself – to eat as much prime, fresh snapper as humanly possible to make room under the bag limit for more. A tough mission, yes, but we had the team for the task.

Another sunrise saw another bottom-bouncing blitzkrieg of quality goldies and jewies, and after more BBQ snapper for breakfast, we began hopping and dropping our way back towards port.

Towards lunch, the sea started turning lumpy, so with eskies full of fillets but a serious dent beginning to appear in the grog supply, we racked the cues. We were exhausted, but quietly content that our mission had been comprehensively accomplished.

I've titled this yarn, 'The demise of the 15-foot snapper tinny', which may seem odd given there is nothing 15-foot about the *Northern Exile*. However, something had become bleedingly obvious to me during my wistful contemplations as we steamed proudly triumphant back to Darwin Harbour. The way I looked at my own tinny had been irrevocably changed. I now found it hard to envisage it as anything more than a barra boat.

Why the hell would I flog around Darwin Harbour, or 60 HP accessible reefs outside, to *maybe* get a feed of pan-size snapper? Pull anchor, bake in the sun, bash knees, back and kidneys to a pulp, clean the putrid bait-baked beast when you get back, then have to fillet fish if you were lucky enough to actually catch some? The true path of wisdom had been revealed to me in a shimmering sunrise delta on that tranquil tropical sea.

Save your shekels, friends and do a fair-dinkum trip every now and then. Sleep in air-con, fish in shade, have someone cook your tucker, fillet your fish and slap a new paternoster on at request. Go to waters you will never reach in your own boat and nail Quality (with a capital 'Q') fish.

The unanimous verdict of all the Gilligans was that it was a cracker of a trip! One that will provide many BBQ yarns for years to come. Yarns that don't require embellishment! Comfortable boat, good crew of blokes, good tucker, fantastic fishing. What more could you want?

And about that once-in-a-lifetime thing? We've already booked for next year.

Politics

Politics is a funny game isn't it, fishos? And when I say funny, I don't mean quaint and amusing like competitive maypole dancing or ride-on lawn-mower racing, I mean funny like, 'You've got to be joking!' or, 'If you didn't laugh you'd throw yourself under a bus,' type funny.

Parliamentary debate seems to be modelled on the kindergarten sandpit rules of engagement: 'Am not!', 'Are so!', 'Well you are, too!' At the end of the day in the assembly, as in the sandpit, the victor rejoices in the tactical genius that has seen him or her maintain a temporary grasp on the high sandy ground, while for the vanquished there is only tears, spat dummies and soiled nappies. The whole infantile tussle just recommences the next day with fresh nappies all round, and the sand-throwing, name-calling and pointless one-upmanship starting all over again.

Politicians don't actually *say* anything any more. During TV interviews, press conferences and highly staged door stops, their mouths move almost continually, but when you sift out the bureaucratese, clichés and obfuscations you are left with four-fifths of bugger all.

Statements from politicians are like those little triangles of Laughing Cow cheese. The bland, generic insipidness of the treat doesn't even register on the palate, and there's no real requirement to chew if you happen to be a bit lazy or slightly disinterested. You can just swallow the thing whole.

Moments later, you are not quite sure what you have just eaten, what it tasted like, or if it was actually a piece of cheese at all – but you do remember it came in some lovely shiny foil with a cute laughing cow on the front!

It doesn't matter which mob has commandeered the coach of state for any particular term, you can be guaranteed that the person behind the wheel who is supposedly driving the bus will be myopic and prone to violent U-turns at the drop of an opinion poll. The first few rows of the vehicle will be populated with faceless co-drivers who all whisper into the driver's ear simultaneous demands for widely divergent changes of course. The driver has no real idea of the route the journey should take or even its ultimate destination, just a grim determination to remain behind the wheel at all costs.

Down the rear of the bus are the bad kids, banished to the back benches due to their membership of a rival gang to that of the current driver. They spend their time heckling and skylarking and giving each other Chinese burns as they plot the putsch that will inevitably see them take their turn down the front manipulating the pedals and levers.

In the middle are the kids being bullied and browbeaten from both sides. They sway to the breeze of factional influence, willing to pledge their transiently wholehearted support to whichever gang appears to have the numerical ascendancy at any given time.

Tim and I had for years denounced the dire state of political debate in this country and the ineptitude of our elected representatives. The stifling of real political progress by the moribund two-party system set our blood boiling and teeth grinding. We abhorred the pathetic charades of the charlatans who cloak themselves in the flag of social advancement and national interest, while pandering to vile, vested interests and lobby group leeches in dodgy back-room deals.

We railed against the entrenched intransigence of the administrative and legislative bureaucracy but realised that dragging our enamel cups back and forth across the bars of the punter barrier keeping the people well away from the corridors of power was not going to bring about the revolutionary change that we desired of the system.

If we were to smash the stinking status quo and stuff the shattered shards right up the fat cat's corpulent clackers, we had to confront the beast from within its odious den. So one Saturday night, with our beer goggles firmly in place but our inspired vision for a better future in sharp focus, the initial spark that would soon be fanned into the roaring ideological inferno of the Tales From The Tinny Fishing First Party burst into being with a righteous incandescence.

It was the humble genesis of a fledgling movement that we believed would ultimately lead the people to a bright and promising future, a new and egalitarian order for fishos, Territorians and other Australians. It was a sobering moment – so we had a couple more sherbets.

The very next day, we embarked on our mission of thrusting the Tales From The Tinny Fishing First Party (henceforth to be known by its catchy acronym of TFTFFP) into the political mainstream. Tim and I had jotted down the core points of our political manifesto on the back of a damp beer coaster late that auspicious Saturday night, just in case we forgot all the best stuff when we sobered up.

The first tactical manoeuvre was the decision that the TFTFFP should contest the forthcoming Northern Territory poll, thereby cementing our power base at a Territory level before sweeping like a cleansing monsoonal storm front through the dank, musty corridors of corruption and mediocrity at a federal level.

We turned our attention to formulating our first policy platform, law and order. We decided 'Crime and punishment' was a better title under which to group our community policing ideas. People seemed to really like the punishment part, in particular.

With the aim of taking on as many erudite and enlightened views as possible to aid in the formulation of a balanced but effective policy, we cast an ear across the dissertations of great and reasoned thinkers on the national stage like Jonesy and Satts. They seemed to think it was a real goer and banged on about it relentlessly, but we needed a local tie-in.

Fortuitously, our resident criminal fraternity came to the rescue by perpetrating a spate of boat-related crimes around Darwin. Cars broken into, vandalised and even torched at boat ramps; fishing gear and whole tinnys being lifted from people's yards; single vehicles parking in designated boat and trailer allocated slots. A heinous crime wave. Political serendipity! We sniffed a TFTFFP vote winner.

The next Saturday morning on The Tinny, we consulted the angling proletariat for their views to help us formulate an inclusive and wide-reaching policy. The response was surprisingly medieval and biblical – the reintroduction of crucifixion and stocks seemed popular. We considered this a bit harsh, but didn't want to play King Canute to the tide of public opinion so we incorporated them into our policy.

Industrial relations was next cab off the rank. We vowed to put into legislation a set of industrial relations innovations under the banner of 'TFTFFP tide choices'. We would introduce a universal rostering system that operated on a lunar cycle instead of the archaic weekly or fortnightly concept. Heavy penalty rates would apply for all employees who were forced to work on good tides. It would also introduce clauses into the unfair dismissal laws that would set in stone the Aussie worker's inalienable right to take 12.5 mental health days per calendar year without fear of retribution, as long as he or she could demonstrate they had been seeking psychological solace through fishing.

Being as what the learned blokes we is and that – edumacation were tops on our ~~pryoritee~~ ~~prioritory~~ ~~piousorority~~ important shit we gotta do list. Under the banner of 'TFTFFP learning stuff and getting more smarter', we gave an iron-clad undertaking that by the end of our first term, every child graduating from primary school in the Northern Territory would be fully conversant with the use of tidal charts and able to competently apply regional variations. Life skills courses would be introduced to high schools offering subjects such as 'Disassembly, servicing and maintenance of overhead bait caster reels' and 'Knot-tying techniques – braid and monofilament'.

To counteract the growing skills shortage in the Territory, new trade schools would be fast-tracked. An emphasis would be placed on critically important skill sets such as aluminium fabrication and welding, and two- and four-stroke marine engineering.

With these three key policy pillars in place, it was time to get down to the business of campaigning. We devised a pork barrelling plan that involved promising a new boat ramp for every electorate in the Territory regardless of whether it had access to water or not. Some of the Central Australian electorates appeared to be a bit marginal by our polling so the campaign committee decided to ratchet up our promise to a two-lane ramp for each of these electorates.

With all this in place, we reckoned we were good to go. It was just down to getting the T-shirts printed and handing out how-to-vote cards, before readying ourselves to move into government house and take up the reins of power.

We went to air with The Tinny on the morning of the election and launched a last-minute saturation campaign blitz that we were confident would be enough to push us over the line and secure office. We came off air exhausted, but confident.

We made our way to our local polling booth where we intended to take each other's photo as we cast our votes. These would be required for inclusion in the victory spread splashed across the front page of the following day's paper. The media had been alerted as to where and when we would be placing our vote, but there must have been some sort of breakdown in communication. We had received no reply from any news outlet, including the ABC.

When we came to be issued with our ballot papers, however, we were horrified to discover that the TFTFFP was nowhere to be found. There followed a furious exchange of accusation and recrimination. 'But I thought you said …', 'You were the one who was supposed to…', ' You bloody idiot', 'Don't call me an idiot you #$%#$##$ …'

Recognising the futility of continuing this tirade, we quickly ran out of abusive steam. There was a bitter pill of cold, harsh reality that required swallowing. This we did, suffering a small but nasty, not quite dry retch as a consequence. We had forgotten to register the party.

We had let down our supporters, our financial backers and the whole disaffected population of the Northern Territory. We would have to wait four long years to implement our bold and visionary policies for the betterment of our beloved NT. We were ashamed, crushed, shattered.

But then, in a blinding flash of inspiration we thought, 'Hang on, isn't there a federal election next year?' We dashed straight to the pub to commence our campaign.

In a factual footnote to the absolute folly of the previous tale, after the Territory election that saw us launch the TFTFFP on air, we got a report from a source whose identity we must guard with our chastity and integrity. (Admittedly, not much to overcome there.)

Our deep throat was involved with electoral returns in the Gove/ Nhulunbuy region. One of his fellow workers approached him during the count with a quizzical look on his face. 'What the hell's this TFTFFP thing, any idea? I'm getting a massive informal vote with ballot cards marked with nothing but a scrawled TFTFFP!'

Our source was a listener and knew exactly what was going on. He restrained a guffaw and resolved to ring us on the quiet as soon as possible, but denied any knowledge of the curious anomaly to his compatriot.

We can't be sure, but we have a pretty solid theory of how this might have eventuated. We often hear from Alcan workers at the Gove Alumina Refinery. The Tinny is often on the radio as the shift bus takes the early crew out to the work site from accommodation in Nhulunbuy. If a whole shift were to hear our electoral pitch one morning and decide it would be a 'hoot' to try and vote us in – you might get just such a result. Who knows?

Politics is a funny game isn't it, fishos?

Stranded – a tale of Shoal Bay

Shoal Bay is immediately to the north-east of Darwin city and a favourite destination for many fishos from both town and the rural area. It produces quality barramundi and jewfish, particularly in the build-up and early run-off, and big muddies abound if you are inclined to drop a pot or two.

Access is relatively easy from Buffalo Creek and Nightcliff ramps in suburban Darwin, or alternatively from private ramps direct into Shoal Bay itself if you are in the know with the landowner. There are many fishing options available to the angler in Shoal Bay with the Howard and Little Howard rivers and Hope Inlet as well as King and Meckitts creeks feeding into it.

The Shoal Bay Rock is a famous monolithic outcrop of, funnily enough, rock, situated inside Hope Inlet. Trolling around the rock can produce big barra and also skinnys (queen fish). Anchoring up on the deep holes at either end of The Rock can produce good snapper and jewies off the bottom. Another option is to get dropped off by boat for a bit of land-based rock-hopping on the outcrop itself. Casting out and dragging big lures back towards The Rock is a favoured method of catching big barra in the build-up.

Unlike most other Top End bays, Shoal has no major rivers or freshwater coastal floodplains feeding it. It's a comparatively shallow waterway with much of the bay becoming exposed sand and mudflat at low tide. One popular Shoal Bay technique is the lock-in. This involves locating a nice hole that will still hold water at the bottom of the tide, and then beaching yourself, or locking-in, as the tide recedes. You can put up a beach umbrella, set up your esky and deckchairs and have a bit of a walk around as you fish the tidal 'hole' left behind. If you happen to lock yourself in to the right hole, the results can be spectacular. Conversely, if you lock in to a fish-free hole, it's a long wait for the tide to come back in and let you move on. In these situations, it can be handy to have a beach cricket set stashed in your boat somewhere.

A lock-in is obviously an intentional stranding, but Shoal Bay is famous for its ability to leave crews high and dry on sand bars when that was definitely not the plan they had in mind.

Because of the expansive and shallow nature of the bay, when a big tide of 7 m or so starts to go, it really goes. If you are fishing the mouths of one of the many feeder creeks emptying into Shoal Bay and leave your run to open water just a couple of casts too late, you will suddenly hear the sound of a motor struggling to push the prop through mud. Shortly after that, you'll find yourself stranded in the middle of a massive sand island with six or eight hours to wait in the beating sun before the tide will relent and float you off again.

It is so common as to be almost a rite of passage around Darwin. If you haven't been stranded in Shoal Bay you're obviously not trying hard enough. Stranding is not a pastime exclusive to boaties either, as Carl from Ludmilla can attest. He had a few hours free one afternoon and so decided he should go for a nice, easy, land-based live bait trip to hunt and gather some fresh fish for dinner. His wife Kelly agreed, but had little faith in him actually doing so.

Carl told her he was going to go downstream from Dixies, the old Shoal Bay boat ramp and would be back by five. He didn't have a newspaper so wasn't sure exactly what the tides were but had a rough idea going on previous tides of the week.

On arrival, he surveyed the scene and decided that upstream actually looked a much better option and so trudged through the mud and scrub for the first big bend in the estuary a couple of hundred metres away. When he got there, once again the tide had defeated him, the water too far out to access.

He continued walking for nearly a kilometre further across the mudflats to Scrubby Creek, and then even further along to an alluring-looking hole just round the bend. Carl threw out the bait net, bagged a few mullet and loaded up a couple of rods. Within minutes, he was smashed by a threadfin salmon. When he eventually landed it he was pleased to see it was a good size too – about 80 cm, he reckoned. 'Nice one, dinner sorted!'

The plan had been to catch one fish and head home, but these plans rarely withstand the adrenaline surge of the initial catch. Carl decided that having nailed the first one so quick, another should only take a second or two and he could head home supremely victorious. A nice barra to make it a mixed grill wouldn't go astray, so he set his mind on achieving that goal.

He had no real idea of the tide and was well aware of the treacherous flows that Shoal Bay was capable of, so he trudged back over the mudflat to Scrubby Creek where he thought he would be able to see the water coming.

Netting a couple more very nice XOS mullet, he lobbed them out and almost instantly got substantial hits on both. Unfortunately, neither hooked up but the ferocity of the strikes had the adrenaline surging again. He ran around madly cast netting for some more mullet to nail one of the big barra he was convinced had smashed the last livies. He was determined to complete his mixed bag.

He got another couple of mullet eventually, but took a number of casts and about 15 minutes to do so. During the excitement of the hits and the subsequent mad scrabble for replacement baits, Carl had taken his eye off the ball – the inexorable advance of the Shoal Bay tide.

After lobbing out his two new baits, he remembered to cast a glance towards the open water and was alarmed at what he saw. He hadn't heard it, hadn't noticed the level rising about him, but about 100 m away was a 50-cm wall of water bearing down on him over the sand bar at a rate of knots.

He frantically packed up his gear and reeled in his baits but by the time he had done so the water was on him. He knew the long way back through the scrub, but opted to make a run at a short cut by returning the way he had come. This very quickly revealed itself to be a bad decision as he needed to work across the current towards the point where he could change tack and head for the car park.

The water was rising so rapidly that by the time he had made it halfway to where he needed to be, it was chest deep. It was running hard and threatening to carry him away so he was forced to make a desperate beeline to the mangroves on the opposite bank.

After a 5-minute breather and a 5-minute session of telling himself what a dickhead he was, he set about working out his next step. Carl hung all his fishing gear high up in trees so as to be able to retrieve it the next day and relinquished his prize thready back to the creek. Striking out through the mangroves towards the narrowest part of the creek, he hoped to be able to find a spot where he could swim across to the car park side.

After 20 minutes of hard yakka and slow progress, as anyone who has walked any distance through mangroves will know it to be, he got to a section of creek that looked narrow enough to have a crack at swimming across.

His long pants and long-sleeve shirt were wet, muddy and very heavy. There was no way he was going to be able to swim with them on, so they got bundled up and stashed in a tree as well. Carl entered the stream and struck out boldly for the far bank. The deceptively swift current gripped him and he was swept downstream. Realising he stood no chance of making it across, he turned and swam hard back towards the bank he had just left.

He hadn't progressed far across the creek in his failed attempt, but he had been washed a good couple of hundred metres downstream by the time he regained the muddy bank. Once again, he was faced with a long hard bash through the mangroves to get to somewhere nearly opposite the ramp. It took over an hour, by which time it was pitch dark.

Carl mentally summed up his situation. He was naked, exhausted, scratched and bruised all over, being hammered by mozzies and sandflies, had no water or food and was stuck in a tropical mangrove swamp for the night. Not too many pluses there.

Smearing himself in stinky mangrove mud, which seemed to provide a marginal deterrent to the mozzies and sandflies, he climbed a tree in the hope that crocs wouldn't do the same. He tried, unsuccessfully, to get as comfortable as possible. It was going to be a long night.

After what seemed like an eternity during which he had completely given up on the prospect of sleep, Carl saw a hopeful glow on the horizon. Soon headlights pierced the darkness around the boat ramp. His mood lifted slightly as he realised salvation might well be at hand.

A bit of mutual cooeeing took place, and it turned out his rescuer was a mate of his, Dave. Carl's wife, Kelly, like most Territory fisho's other halves took, 'I'll be home by five!' to mean any time between six and eight. When Carl hadn't turned up by nine, she called Dave, who had just driven back into town from Jabiru. He reassured her it was probably just a car breakdown, and went out to see if a tow was required.

Dave was now perched on the bank of the creek on the boat ramp side with a big torch. The water was still way too high to make a safe crossing, he reckoned. He wasn't all that keen on getting too close to the water's edge to make an accurate assessment of the water's depth – there was a very good chance a big, hungry handbag could be hanging around.

Dave had a newspaper in the car and therefore accurate tide times. Carl calculated that he should be right to come across by about midnight. Dave continued warning him off until about 1 am, still considering it to be too deep. By then, Carl wasn't taking 'stay' for an answer. He'd had nothing to eat or drink for hours, the skin was peeling off his toes, he ached and stung and was on the edge of insanity with mozzie bites.

He struck out towards the light and freedom, obviously cutting a fine figure in the moonlight – totally nude and covered in mud and a rich variety of welts as he entered the creek. As it turned out, the water didn't even reach his knees and he strolled casually across to salvation. He could have made the crossing hours earlier.

He returned to his car and liberated a spare key wired up underneath, only to find that he had left the lights on and the battery was flat as a tack. This would really have been the last straw if he was there on his own. He thanked his lucky stars that Dave had been back in town and available as he pulled jumper leads from his car.

Carl made himself a firm resolve that in future, 'One fish and go home,' would really mean, 'One. Fish. And. Go. Home!'

Books 'n' barra

As you fold closed the back cover of this book at the completion of this chapter, I hope the delicately daubed mental images of our magnificent Top End landscape, the glimpses afforded into the unique Territory character and lifestyle all bound together with my often delusional freeform ramblings, has provided you with the stuff of continued, considered contemplation and amused recollection.

Another possible outcome at the same folding of the back cover is to throw the completed book down in disgust with a derisive snort and demand, 'What the hell was that piece of drivel?'

Either way, please join me for one last literary meandering. As we approach the conclusion of this book that has been devoted in no small part to the barramundi, let me pose the question, 'Are books better than barra?'

WordStorm is the Top End's biennial writers' festival that traditionally culminates in a comedy debate. A mix of guest authors and local scribes make up the opposing panels of the debate and the subject is always of a literary nature, predictably enough.

Given my propensity to pen and pontificate on a piscatorial theme, when the debate topic was revealed to be 'That books are better than barra,' I was seen as a natural advocate for the negative case and press-ganged into service.

What follows is an adaptation of my argument for the negative case, that barra *are* in fact better than books. I hope it can help clear up any lingering confusion you may have regarding the topic, but quite honestly doubt that it will do anything of the sort.

Firstly, to set the scene, picture yourself in a balmy beer garden at the Mandorah Hotel, a 20-minute ferry ride across the harbour from Darwin's Cullen Bay, or alternatively a 150-km drive, partially over corrugated dirt. A delightful breeze wafts in off the harbour as I nervously run through my presentation, terrified at the prospect of verbally jousting with fair dinkum authors who know lots of words 'n' that.

The audience is a mix of bookish types, arty-farty literati, rough-head fishos, entertainment-starved Darwinites in search of a giggle and a fair smattering of locals (both feral and Mandorah high society). The unifying trait is that they are all having either a few quiet ones, or a big mob of loud ones in preparation for proceedings.

Soon the teams take the stage and verbal hostilities commence. All other speakers make their impassioned pleas and state the undeniable logic of their arguments. The judging panel and the audience seem to be teetering indecisively as my turn comes as final speaker to try and sweep the tide of public opinion in our favour and claim a glorious victory not only for the negative team, but the illiterates and fishermen of the Top End – a pairing that has significant commonalities.

I stride to the rostrum confidently trying to exude an aura of authoritative self-assuredness. Retrieving a fresh barra caught earlier that day from an esky hidden behind our table, I hold it aloft for all to see and launch into my pitch …

Lates calcarifer – the mighty barramundi. Behold its marine magnificence! The sleekly streamlined front-end featuring the distinctively scooped dorsal head profile, the elongated jawline to facilitate the operation of the famously cavernous bucket mouth, the shimmering silver sheen of its powerful flanks. Let's face it, this little baby ticks all the boxes of design excellence – form, function, fight and fillet. All in one perfect piscatorial package.

If Ferrari were ever to engineer an underwater vehicle they would surely call it 'the barramundi' and use the beautiful flowing lines of the mighty *calcarifer* to shape the exterior design.

'Barramundi', as a possible model name, has the added advantage for the Italians of already ending with the letter 'i', though the barra itself may well actually resent the implied slur on its temperament that sharing a name with a piece of Italian engineering may infer.

This, on the other hand, is a book. (I reach into the same esky but this time retrieve a fairly plain hard-cover book dripping with faux barra slime.) A rectangular prism comprising myriad, bound sheets of printed paper. It boasts a non-descript hard cover, contains 62 274 words divided into discrete chapters banging on about … well, I dunno what. And you know what? There's absolutely nothing here that really entices me to try and find out. (I shake the book in the general direction of the opposition benches, spraying them with gobs of the barra slime.)

Highly overrated in my book – books, that is. For a start, they don't keep well on ice. (A long snotty dag of slime drips to the stage.) But don't get me wrong. I'm not one of those philistonians who blindly bag something they don't understand out of simple ignorance and fear.

Oh no, no, no. My judgement is made from a position of informed awareness. I had a book once – read it too! It came with my sounder. As I said, highly overrated. The premise was preposterous, the characterisation clichéd and two dimensional at best, the plot development tortured, and the dialogue? Enough said …

Then, when you got a few chapters in – just as it started to gather some momentum – the whole yarn starts all over again in French, then Korean and Arabic. Now whose ridiculous idea was that! Must give you mob the screaming shits to have to do that all the time. Fair dinkum! (Addressed to all authors on both panels.)

Books are overrated, as opposed to the barra, which should by rights be x-rated, because they are so undeniably damn sexy! Those highly reflective bedroom eyes, the coquettish come-hither smile and flick of the tail as it spits your lure back at you. Always playing hard to get.

And speaking of sex, what about the old love tackle switcheroo the barra manages to pull off? Sequentially hermaphroditic. Even sounds sexy just saying it, don't ya reckon?

Books are overrated. A book is a book is a book, just big mobs of words and stuff. Whereas the barramundi is so much more than just a fish. It is the source of myth, fable and conjecture. The pursuit of the barra is a poignant metaphor for life's everyday struggle.

The barramundi is accepted as an alternative form of currency in the Northern Territory nearly as readily as a slab of beer. Fillets of barra can form payment for the loan of a mate's trailer, as taxi fare if you need a lift somewhere when fiscally challenged, or as payment for the previously mentioned universally accepted quasi-currency of beer!

Barramundi fillets have even been used in attempts to bribe the wallopers on occasion, offered as exchange for a blind eye being turned to a matter of un-roadworthiness or excess in speed. Now the fine Northern Territory constabulary had no part of this, of course, but can you ever imagine the alternative scenario?

Woo-woo-woo-woo! (Vocal sound effects are accompanied by an opening and closing hand above the head in an amateurish theatrical representation of police lights and siren.)

'Excuse me, sir. Is there any reason for you to be towing your boat containing two paralytic fishermen and an inflatable sex doll, erratically and at high speed at 1 am through the Botanic Gardens?'

Driver replies, 'Sorry, officer. That roundabout at Darwin High stuffs me up every time but look, I'm sure we can come to an arrangement here. I just happen to have a well-thumbed 2nd edition of *The Female Eunuch* in the glove box. You walk away with that, I drive away quietly with the boat and me mates, and we forget the whole silly thing. Whaddyareckon?'

Me thinks not.

Books are overrated. They are also possibly damaging to your mental health and emotional wellbeing, creating worlds of construct, fantasy and delusion.

This is confusing and dangerous territory to simple folk such as fishos, but also, it seems, great minds. The venerated French thinker, philosopher and writer, Voltaire, claimed 'the multitude of books is making us ignorant'. Right on, Volley! Too many sets of books spells trouble, that's for sure – just ask Bernie Madoff, Glenn Wheatley or the Melbourne Storm.

Books have long been used in a disciplinarian fashion by stern librarians and tyrannical teachers – a device to refocus a fractious group's wandering attention. (I slam the book down very loudly onto the corner of the opposition table with an accompanying spray of slime.) Does the job I suppose.

But if you really want to stop a conversation dead and command undivided attention, the barra reigns supreme – BOOF! (A very loud, technically enhanced recording of a barra 'boof' played through the PA shocks the audience and debaters alike.)

Now that I have your attention, it's high time I took apart the tawdry tissue of lies put forward by my myopic cardigan-wearing opponents opposite. Barra are better than books because – as ably demonstrated by my slightly nauseous but obviously dedicated colleague Phillip Gwynne – you cannot eat a book – BOOF! (My point is punctuated once again with loud PA assistance.)

You cannot stuff and mount a book you were proud of reading – BOOF!

You cannot continue reading after consuming ten cans of beer and eight bongs of bush weed – BOOF!

Barramundi tourism is a huge money-spinner for the Territory's coffers. You could almost say that barra balance the budgetary books. Library tourism, however, is non-existent – BOOF!

You are not gonna ring up a mate on a quiet Sunday arvo and suggest you get together for a bit of a read – BOOF!

You are not gonna go to the effort of putting in the gammin' symptomatic groundwork the day before, then ring up the boss and take a sickie just so that you can stay home and read a book – BOOF!

You cannot use a frozen book as a weapon – BOOF!

There is no way you would get up at 3 am to bash over 500 km of corrugations to get to a mozzie-infested library on the off-chance that you might possibly be able to borrow a book – BOOF! BOOF! BOOF!

In summary, I called for argumentative assistance from The Tinny listeners on the website last week (abc.net.au/tinny). Allison, a fairly forthright Territory girl replied, 'I've never had an orgasm reading a book, Rob, but when I landed that 90-cm barra …' (SFX of a woman in the throes of considerable ecstasy plays through the PA.)

The negative rests its case! (Thunderous applause from the audience ensues.)

The tradition of the WordStorm comedy debate is that the team arguing for the literary premise always wins. This was also the case on this occasion, but my teammates and I held our heads high in the certain knowledge that the intellectual, emotional and moral victories were ours. The official title of winner was irrelevant.

And so, as it comes time to wind up my literary ramblings on this particular outing, I shall refrain from drawing out proceedings with a prolonged epilogue. I shall simply state that barra are better than books, even this one, and sign off somewhat predictably with the utilitarian conversational catch-all –

Get a mullet up ya !